A Genealogy of
Violence and Religion

T0374897

Girard's understanding of the relationship between religion and violence has never been more timely and relevant than it is now, yet his thought remains largely inaccessible to educated amateurs. Murphy's book is a loving (and therefore critical) attempt to make his essential ideas intelligible to a broad audience. This is also a most unusual book. It is engaging and accessible, but intellectually and morally deep. Murphy wears his scholarship lightly, but his command of the relevant research is beyond question. It is a dialogue, and in an old Talmudic trick, it brings together great thinkers from across the centuries in fitting, convivial settings, where they speak face-to-face as existing individuals. Murphy is a polymath, and one of the book's many pleasures is the way it gently teaches us about the ideas and insights of the speakers besides Girard. Not only does it raise fundamental questions, it furnishes readers with the resources to come up with their own answers. One could hardly ask for more in a short book! I think this will be a favorite entryway into Girard's thought for years to come.

JACOB HOWLAND
McFarlin Professor of Philosophy, University of Tulsa

Of the many books on René Girard, Jim Murphy's is unique because it is cast as a series of symposia in which Girard enters into conversation with a broad range of figures from the Western canon—from Socrates to Sigmund Freud—who have thought about desire, worship, violence, and beauty. The imagined conversations are broad and deep, contentious and full of humor. The book is fun, a rollicking good read. Though Murphy lets others do the talking, his own keen mind shows through. Neither a Girard acolyte nor someone who dismisses Girard out of hand, Murphy finds Girard and the whole range of issues he brings to light well worth a good argument. Short and accessible for students, this book would be great for use in the classroom.

DR. WILLIAM T. CAVANAUGH
Professor, DePaul University, Director,
Center for World Catholicism and Intercultural Theology

This is one of the best scholarly works I have read on Girard. Marshalling a vast backstory to Girard's work, and with enviable lucidity, Murphy helps us to understand how Girard's work belongs within a larger and older set of problems besides those he defines for himself. This book breaks Girard's thought out of the isolation often imposed on it and adds a crucial depth dimension. It would make a great text on the undergraduate level, as an introduction not just to Girard and the issues he raises, but to lots of other thinkers as well. Their voices and their engagement with each other are laid out in a fair and critical way, in language that is clear and accessible. Anyone who takes seriously Girard's ambition to reanimate the "human sciences" or the political implications of his thought will appreciate it.

JOHN RANIERI
Department of Philosophy, Seton Hall University

This is a creative, well-written, interesting, and genuinely thought-provoking book. I liked it a lot, and I'm impressed by the amount of material incorporated here, and the skill with which Murphy weaves conversations. *A Genealogy of Violence and Religion* is an excellent introduction to some of the ways in which Girard's work might be criticized. Murphy picks up on some of the important questions Girard leaves unresolved, especially with regard to violence and pacifism. Based on my reading of Girard and some conversations I've had with him, my impression is that the way Murphy has Girard responding to his interlocutors is almost always on target.

STEPHEN GARDNER
Department of Philosophy, University of Tulsa

In Memoriam

Joseph Francis Daschbach: 1937–2013

A Genealogy of
Violence and Religion

René Girard in Dialogue

James Bernard Murphy

sussex
ACADEMIC
PRESS
Brighton • Chicago • Toronto

2 4 6 8 10 9 7 5 3 1

First published 2018, in Great Britain by
SUSSEX ACADEMIC PRESS
PO Box 139
Eastbourne BN24 9BP

Distributed in the United States of America by
SUSSEX ACADEMIC PRESS
Independent Publishers Group
814 N. Franklin Street, Chicago, IL 60610

British Library Cataloguing in Publication Data
A CIP catalogue record for this book is available from the British Library.

Library of Congress Cataloging-in-Publication Data
Names: Murphy, James Bernard, 1958– author.
Title: A genealogy of violence and religion : René Girard in dialogue / James Bernard Murphy.
Description: Portland, Oregon : Sussex Academic Press, 2018. | Includes bibliographical references and index.
Identifiers: LCCN 2018001612 | ISBN 9781845199289 (pbk : alk. paper)
Subjects: LCSH: Violence—Religious aspects. | Violence. | Philosophy— Philosophy. | Girard, René, 1923–2015.
Classification: LCC BL65.V55 M86 2018 | DDC 201/.76332—dc23
LC record available at https://lccn.loc.gov/2018001612

Typeset & designed by Sussex Academic Press, Brighton & Eastbourne.
Printed and bound by CPI Group (UK) Ltd, Croydon, CR0 4YY

Contents

Preface
Why Girard?
Why Dialogue?

René Girard (1923–2015) has been described as the Darwin of the human sciences for his seminal theories of violence and religion. Where does violence come from? Is there an instinct for aggression? Or does violence emerge from social rivalry? How does violence relate to religion? When people think of religion and violence, they usually think of religion as a cause of violence. In the wake of contemporary militant Islam, a literature has emerged exploring the claim that religion is an important cause of violence. After all, religious rhetoric and especially religious rituals, such as ritual sacrifice, are steeped in symbolic or actual blood and killing. And some religions, even religions based on love, are known to inspire a great deal of hatred. Certainly, history shows much violent conflict waged in the name of religion, whatever its true causes.

In the nineteenth century, some scholars, observing the same correlation between religion and violence, argued for a different causal relation. They argued that it was violence that gave rise to religion. In this view, religious language and practices are full of violence because their function is to sublimate and to control human impulses, including violent impulses. William Robertson Smith and Gilbert Murray, for example, argued in different ways that religion arose from rituals associated with hunting. These scholars thought of violence as a primordial part of the human condition, like sex and death. From a broadly anthropological perspective, religious rituals appear as ways to routinize and hence normalize dangerous impulses and fearful transitions of human life. For example, rites of initiation and of passage serve to normalize sexual impulses and the fear of crossing various thresholds in life. Similarly, rites of sacrifice and of communal meals serve to sublimate and normalize violent impulses. Sigmund Freud provided a classic and seminal account of the view that violence gave rise to religion in his *Totem and Taboo*. Emile Durkheim and his French students argued that sacrifice was the basis of religion and that it served to produce social harmony. That violence might in some respects give rise to religion is, of course, compatible with the possibility that in other respects religion also causes violence.

René Girard was the most eminent recent scholar to argue that violence is the origin of religion. Yet Girard was equally interested in the origins of violence itself and offered a fascinating social-psychological theory of violence. He described his own life's work of more than five decades as simply exploring the implications of "a single, extremely dense insight." What was that dense insight? From reading the novels of Cervantes, Stendhal, and Dostoevsky, Girard came to believe that we desire something only when we notice that someone else desired it first. Unlike other animals, human beings are not hardwired to desire only a fixed set of objects; we learn what to desire from other people. In the classic French triangle, a man desires a woman only because another man also desires her. This imitative or what Girard calls "mimetic" desire leads inexorably to rivalry, conflict, and violence. These conflicts spread by mimetic contagion until someone selects a scapegoat, who is blamed for all the violence. The community then comes together in harmony around the project of killing the scapegoat. The scapegoat often then comes to be treated as sacred because its death saved the community from a crisis of contagious violence. What does this have to do with religion? In Girard's account, religious ritual, especially sacrifice, serves both to commemorate and to recreate the social harmony realized by the murder of the scapegoat. As he began to study the Bible, however, Girard came to believe that biblical religion, especially Christianity, offers a profound critique of the whole logic of scapegoating and, therefore, a critique of ritual sacrifice. Girard later argued that Christianity is the enemy of all religion since religion is based on sacrificial violence.

Unpacking this one dense insight thus led Girard into many different disciplines, including psychology, anthropology, literary studies, sociology, and biblical studies. Today, we live in an academic world of hyper-specialization in which we know more and more about less and less—until finally we shall know everything about nothing. Dismayed by these trends, scholars are increasingly asking: Where are today's grand theorists of the human sciences? Who is the Karl Marx, Sigmund Freud, Max Weber, or Emile Durkheim of our time? Is grand theory in the human sciences still even possible? Although many of the ideas of these famous theorists have not survived critical scrutiny, each of them displayed grandeur of vision and an intellectual imagination especially rare today. I think René Girard also displays the grandeur and the imagination we associate with the great theorists of the recent past. Although Girard rejected the idea that he had developed a Girardian system comparable to Marxism or Freudianism, his "dense insight" offers us a unified perspective on human life encompassing psychology, literature, sociology, anthropology, and religion. Like many people, I find his project exciting. Knowledge is vast and life is short: what a thrill to discover what could be a key to unlock the storehouse or a thread to lead us through the labyrinth.

Who was René Noël Théophile Girard? He was born on Christmas Day, 1923, in Avignon, France. His father was a local archivist, and René followed suit by pursuing historical training in medieval studies in Paris. In 1947, however, René Girard enrolled in the doctoral program in history at Indiana University, where he studied American views of France during the Second World War. Although Girard would live and teach in the United States for more than fifty years, he continued to write almost all his books in French. He often said that America gave him the precious freedom to pursue his interdisciplinary research—a freedom Girard used to become a wide-ranging French intellectual rather than an American-style academic. Each of his major books marks a new transgression of disciplinary boundaries. In *Deceit, Desire and the Novel* (1961; English, 1966), Girard studies "triangular desire" in literary writers from Cervantes to Proust. His 1972 book *Violence and the Sacred* (English, 1977) is a study of scape-goating and sacrifice in the anthropology and psychology of religion. In 1978, he turned to biblical studies in *Things Hidden Since the Foundation of the World* (English, 1987). Finally, he engaged Carl von Clausewitz's account of conflict and war in his *Battling to the End: Conversations with Benoît Chantre* (English, 2010). Despite living most of his life in America, Girard's primary intellectual milieu remained French, from the sociologists, Gabriel Tarde, Gustave Le Bon, and Emile Durkheim, to the philosophers, Jean-Paul Sartre and Jacques Derrida, and anthropologist Claude Lévi-Strauss. He was elected to the Académie Française in 2005, confirming his place in the French intellectual pantheon.

What is most striking about the thought of René Girard is its blending of scientific theorizing and moral passion. He aspires to be both a Louis Pasteur by developing an etiology of contagious violence and an Emile Zola by denouncing the human proclivity to violence, scapegoating, and sacrifice. Girard often emphasizes his commitment to scientific rigor and objectivity while at the same time freely using very strong moral language to damn and to praise. No one has accused him of moral sentimentality about the human condition: he argues that human beings are fundamentally prone to dangerous rivalries and destructive cycles of revenge, retalia-tion, and vendetta; the only thing that makes social life possible is the sacred violence whereby the anarchic war of all against all becomes a war of all against one. All religions, all societies, and all cultures arise from the unity of a lynch mob. To him, the only cure for contagious social violence is the ritu-alized violence of scapegoating and sacrifice—until, that is, Jesus's example of perfect nonviolence finally reveals how we can escape the horrible choice between anarchic and sacred violence. Girard asks us to renounce violence after showing us that violence is rooted in human desire itself. From 1978 until the end of his life, Girard repeatedly posed this apocalyptic dilemma: either we renounce all violence or we face self-destruction.

Girard's moral condemnation of violence is difficult to square with his scientific view that sacred violence and the violence of legal punishment function to control chaotic violence. As a scientist, Girard explains how sacred violence regulates and limits mimetic violence, but as a moralist and a Christian, Girard condemns violence. He frequently describes his own work as providing the truth necessary to make war on violence. He does not underestimate his opponent: "Violence is a terrible adversary, since it always wins." Girard is clear that violence does not emerge from individual choice; rather, it emerges from social situations of triangular desire. But if violence does not emerge from individual choice, then how can individuals be expected to renounce violence? His scientific functionalism seems to undermine the moral individualism and personal responsibility required for the renunciation of violence. We see a similar paradox in the thought of Karl Marx, whose social theory also combines scientific aspiration with fierce moral passion. Marx's theory of history is profoundly deterministic: the logic of historical change seems utterly indifferent to voluntary revolutionary action. If history follows its own inexorable laws, why does Marx call for a deliberate human effort to attempt to change history? Marx devoted his life to the study of capitalism, yet he is regarded as the chief theoretician of communism. Similarly, Girard devoted his life to the study of violence, yet he is now regarded as the chief theoretician of pacifism. Marx and Girard were focused on diagnosis; their many followers look to them for remedies.

In Girard's case, if violence has its own social logic far removed from the ways in which individuals conceptualize their own moral choices, then how can he ask us to renounce violence? Girard's moral passion always coexisted with his scientific theorizing; from his earliest work, he expressed horror at the violence endemic to human life. Fairly early in his intellectual career he returned to the Catholic faith of his childhood and he claimed that his scientific theory of violence led him to see the truth of Christianity. However, his critics have argued that he instead merely turned his social theory into an instrument of Christian apologetics. In my view, the question of the relation of his Christianity to his scholarship is only one aspect of the more fundamental question of the relation of his moral passion to his scientific functionalism. Many pacifists look to Girard for a theoretical foundation for their peace-making. Are they looking in the right place? In my "Concluding Reflections on Violence," I shall briefly explore the relation of Girard's scientific theory to his moral condemnations of violence.

Girard's scholarship possesses an astonishing degree of unity, especially considering that he developed the implications of his one dense insight over a period of more than fifty years. Naturally, there were subtle developments in his thought and some shifts of emphasis. In particular, Girard's engagement with the Bible, beginning with his book *Things Hidden Since the Foundation of the World* (1978), led him for the first time to renounce all violence. But Girard explicitly repudiated only one aspect of his earlier thought and that was his earlier denial that the death of Jesus could be described in any way as self-sacrifice. Hence, with this one exception, I shall treat his thought as a whole because that is how Girard saw it.

Girard's work has provoked voluminous commentary in thousands of articles and hundreds of books. What accounts for such an immense Girard industry? Perhaps it is because his work combines a maximum of provocative ideas with a minimum of expository rigor. How can one justify yet another book about Girard? After all, there are already several excellent expositions of Girard's thought, especially by Chris Fleming, Michael Kirwan, and Wolfgang Palaver. These books are sympathetic to Girard's project and explain his ideas with more philosophical rigor than we find in Girard himself. Gil Bailie has written an influential book, *Violence Unveiled: Humanity at the Crossroads*, which both explains Girard's ideas and develops them further. Bailie's book has inspired an extensive literature of neo-Girardian theorizing that reaches into all aspects of human culture. More critical of Girard is Paisley Livingston's excellent book-length philosophical critique of Girard's theory of mimetic desire, *Models of Desire: René Girard and the Psychology of Mimesis*.

My goal is neither to explain Girard's ideas nor to criticize them. Instead, I want the reader to be able to compare Girard's ideas with the competing ideas of other major thinkers. How do Girard's theories of literature, desire, crowds, and sacrifice compare with rival theories? To find out, I provide a set of transcripts of Girard's dialogues and debates with Aristotle, Immanuel Kant, Leo Tolstoy, Sigmund Freud, Simone Weil, Elias Canetti, Joseph de Maistre, William James, and other important thinkers and scholars. Although Girard's expositors and his critics also compare his ideas with those of other thinkers, my set of dialogues permits a more thorough and rigorous set of comparisons. Rather than assessing the strengths and weaknesses of Girard's thought myself, I let readers make the assessment themselves. Most importantly, I let Girard defend himself against a wide range of attacks. These conversations are not focused on Girard himself but rather on the fundamental questions that he asks. Whatever we may think about the merits of Girard's answers, we can agree that he asks great questions.

This book begins with a parable illustrating Girard's account of the birth of religion. My aim in this parable is to dramatize Girard's ideas in a persuasive and sympathetic manner. I believe that his ideas are more compelling in the form of a story than in the usual potted summary. I then permit Girard and his interlocutors to discuss the question of why we read literature, the question of what is mimetic desire, the question of why there are scapegoats and, finally, the question of what is the meaning of sacrifice. I conclude with some reflections on the concept of violence in Girard's thought and beyond.

Too often in our analysis of other writers, we caricature them by focusing on the inadequacies of their verbal formulations. Yet often the words of a given thinker are only the visible tip of a much deeper and more nuanced intellectual position— a position which permits of better or worse verbal articulation. Through dialogue, we are able to surface more of the underlying position of the interlocutors by enabling them to explain and defend their views. Each character in a dialogue has more motivation to explain his or her thoughts than any detached scholar or critic. Instead of straw men, dialogues give us real, unpredictable, flesh-and-blood characters. In a scholarly monologue, the author attempts to seduce, hector, or persuade the reader to accept a particular point of view—often enough by ignoring or caricaturing alternative views. As a reader of scholarly argument, I often sense that the author is more bent on gaining my assent than illuminating my understanding. Put simply, I feel bullied. When reading dialogues, by contrast, I feel freer to entertain a variety of points of view, to mix and match, and to suspend final judgment.

Nonetheless, dialogues impose unique burdens upon readers. In a scholarly monograph, the author does most of the work by synthesizing and evaluating a range of views before offering his or her own account. In a dialogue, the reader is challenged to synthesize and to evaluate a wide range of views, without being told what to think. A monograph produces a take-it-or-leave-it conclusion; a dialogue invites the reader to come to his or her own conclusion. I ask the reader of this book to enjoy the play of ideas and to take up the challenge of thinking for yourself about these important matters.

My hope is that these dialogues are both entertaining and illuminating. Through these conversations a reader is able to enjoy a range of intellectual perspectives that would not be possible in a book by one author. In my view, Girard invites such a dialogical treatment. His best books are the extended interviews or conversations in which his ideas unfold dialogically, such as *Things Hidden Since the Foundation of the World*; *When These Things Begin*; *Evolution and Conversion*; *Christianity, Truth, and Weakening Faith*; and *Battling to the End*. Girard was a better talker than he was a writer, so in this book I let him talk. René Girard the man has died; in these dialogues, René Girard the thinker lives on.

Dramatis Personae
(in order of appearance)

Cole Porter (1891–1964): Widely regarded as the greatest of American songwriters, Cole Porter remains famous for his charming melodies and catchy lyrics—or is it for his catchy melodies and charming lyrics? As a classically-trained composer and a lover of literature, Porter is the ideal master of ceremonies.

Socrates (469–399 BC): An ancient Athenian lover of wisdom who founded Western moral and political philosophy. A legendary talker, Socrates believed that knowledge was best pursued through living dialogue and debate rather than through the tedious monologue of treatises. Because he never wrote anything, his views have become known to us mainly through the written dialogues of his student, Plato. Socrates was executed in 399 BC, proving the adage "publish or perish."

Oscar Wilde (1854–1900): A flamboyantly brilliant and witty Irish dramatist, poet, and novelist who is quoted more often than any English writer since Shakespeare. A champion of "art for art's sake" in the face of Victorian moralizing, Wilde was persecuted for his homosexual liaisons, suffering imprisonment and early death.

Simone Weil (1909–1943): A Jewish philosopher and anarchist who was also a Catholic-Christian mystic. Weil rejected the bourgeois comfort of her family and intellectual milieu in order to experience the suffering of factory workers, peasants, and soldiers. Her meditations on literature and intellectual study as paths to God are modern classics.

René Girard (1923–2015): Described as the Darwin of the human sciences, Girard was a French literary theorist, anthropologist, and social psychologist who spent most of his life teaching and writing in the United States. Girard is best known for his theories of the scientific value of great literature, the concept of mimetic desire, the social-psychology of scapegoating, and the nature of biblical sacrifice.

Aristotle (384–322 BC): An ancient Greek philosopher and a student of Plato's. Aristotle's thirty philosophical and scientific treatises dominated higher education for two thousand years, making him "the master of those who know." Aristotle invented the discipline of literary criticism, arguing that literary narratives imitate or represent human life. In other words, human lives are comic, tragic, romantic, or farcical just like our dramas.

Immanuel Kant (1724–1804): Prussian philosopher and champion of the German Enlightenment ("Dare to know!"). Kant is famous for his theories of morality and art in relation to rational knowledge. He emphasized the contrast between the beautiful and the sublime in our experience of art.

Sigmund Freud (1856–1939): Viennese neurologist and founder of psychoanalysis, Freud developed influential psychological theories of literature, religion, crowds, and violence. Freud's view that violence gives rise to religion deeply influenced the work of René Girard.

Leo Tolstoy (1828–1910): Russian novelist, Christian anarchist, and moral philosopher. Author of two of the greatest novels of all time, *War and Peace* and *Anna Karenina*, Tolstoy later repudiated these works as immoral. In his philosophical writings on art, he insisted that all good works of art create bonds of love across all social classes.

William James (1842–1910): American philosopher and psychologist; older brother of novelist Henry James. Often called the father of American philosophical pragmatism and the founder of scientific psychology in the United States. James was a pioneering scholar of religious experience, emotion, and violence.

Gordon Allport (1897–1967): Leading American researcher in both personality psychology and social psychology. Allport pioneered the scientific study of personality traits which he used to explain both individual and social behavior. Brother of psychologist Floyd Henry Allport, Gordon Allport published influential studies of prejudice, rumor, and scapegoating.

Elias Canetti (1905–1994): Descended from Spanish Jews, Canetti was a Bulgarian-born, Viennese intellectual who wrote in German. His works include novels, memoirs, dramas, and treatises on social theory—for which he received the Nobel Prize in Literature in 1981. As a café intellectual in central Europe between the wars, Canetti experienced firsthand the destructive violence of crowds, leading to his magisterial study of crowd psychology and sociology.

John Milbank (1952–present): Anglican Christian theologian and founder of "radical orthodoxy" in contemporary Christian thought. Milbank has written extensively about political theology, Christian social theory, and Christian ethics. He has also written about theories of sacrifice, including the theory of René Girard.

Joseph de Maistre (1753–1821): French-speaking Savoyard nobleman, diplomat, and writer who was born in northern Italy and lived for many years in Russia. An intellectual leader of the Catholic Counter-Enlightenment, Maistre wrote very influential polemics defending the "trinity" of Pope, King, and Hangman. Maistre is today best known for his theories of violence and religion as the foundations of social order: "All grandeur, all power, all subordination to authority rests upon the executioner."

Jacob Milgrom (1923–2010): American biblical scholar and Conservative rabbi who is best known for his authoritative commentaries upon the book of Leviticus and its laws of ritual sacrifice.

Robert Daly (1933–present): Professor Emeritus of Theology at Boston College. Father Daly is a Jesuit priest and scholar of biblical ideas of sacrifice. He has written extensively upon the Christian theology of sacrifice in relation to the anthropology of René Girard.

CHAPTER ONE

Living Water:
A Parable

Whosoever drinketh of this water shall thirst again: But whosoever drinketh of the water that I shall give him shall never thirst; but the water that I shall give him shall be in him a well of water springing up into everlasting life. JOHN 4:13–14

My name is Joseph Daschbach, and I am a Catholic priest. I tell this story so that future generations will understand the terrible events that befell my community. Yes, we were under the pressure of drought, but mere scarcity does not begin to explain our ordeal. Each of us seemed to want only what belonged to his or her neighbor. No one was satisfied with what he already possessed. Soon, we were locked into the most absurd and sometimes deadly rivalries. I saw a contagion of violence sweep our once placid village, like a plague. I found myself carried away by the raging torrents of violent passion. Each of us wants to believe that we would keep our heads while everyone else is losing theirs. I was sure that I would remain the calm center of a raging hurricane. Well, perhaps you could have remained calm, but I certainly did not. Nothing is as humiliating as finding yourself shaken like a rag doll by passions you know to be totally irrational. Let me simply tell you what I saw and heard during these past few months, and you can try to explain it for yourself. None of us wanted to go where these events took us. We were caught in some diabolical mechanism which compelled us to escalate our conflicts to catastrophic extremes. What is even more bizarre—speaking as a Catholic priest—is that we witnessed the birth of a new religious cult. I can only wonder: Do all religions emerge from the kind of violence we experienced?

Today, we live in a world of intense national rivalry, combined with the destructive power of nuclear weapons. This means that we face an apocalyptic choice between the renunciation of violence and the total annihilation of the human species. I am convinced that only a deep conversion of every human heart to nonviolence would prevent conflicts from escalating to the extremes of mutually assured destruction. And though the conflagration of violence that beset my village did not rise to the level of atomic war, it embodied the same irrational rivalries and mindless escalation.

You may wonder how I could know all these intimate stories. Well, there is no window on human nature quite like the confessional. And there is no crime quite like breaking the seal of the confessional, so I have changed the names to protect the guilty.

"Hey, Essau, what are you doing outside in the daylight? Aren't you afraid of the curfew?"

"Cut the crap, Jacob, or I'll ask you the same questions. Come watch these ants."

A few droplets of moisture had congealed overnight on the parched mud of the riverbed.

Essau pointed out an ant that was pushing a ball of water like a giant beach ball; somehow the surface tension kept the water intact. But soon other ants were attempting to push the same droplet in contrary directions.

"I thought ants were super-cooperative? Don't they all share the same hive-brain? Aren't members of a colony all just parts of one organism?"

"Maybe they belong to different colonies. But in this heat, who wants to be cooperative?"

Now the ants were fighting each other, and the droplet burst; immediately, it was swallowed up by the thirsty Earth. Essau focused the sunlight with his magnifying glass and began to incinerate the hapless ants. Tiny plumes of smoke arose from the burnt offerings.

"I am Lord of the Ants."

Jacob grabbed the glass from Essau's hand. "We'll see who is Lord."

At the town meeting that night, the gymnasium was over-flowing. The drought had ensured that there would be no shortage of passion or opinion at our meetings. The town manager, Nehemiah, called the meeting to order, but the tense murmuring continued, sotto voce. The body odor wafting up from the crowd was evenly distributed by the ceiling fans.

Samuel rose to speak: "Ever since the college moved north to our Canadian provinces, there have been doubts about the future of our beloved village. True, our village is older than the college and can live without her, but we have been struggling to attract other employers here. Our town misses its gown. Why don't we just move our village to Canada as well? We could then reunite with our separated spouse."

"Sam," said Nehemiah, "your alma mater has abandoned us. Time to grow up. We have already debated and decided this issue. Now let's move on, figuratively speaking."

Naomi raised her hand to speak: "I want to talk about our gardens. People have been stealing flowers from my raised beds under cover of daylight. What can we do about this?"

Mock sighs could be heard throughout the room, and Ruth burst out: "Naomi, quit complaining. The rest of us are stuck with cactus gardens. At least you have water for your garden. I have not had a proper shower in five years. In fact, why don't we end the sale of nonessential water? Seeing the lush gardens of our rich neighbors brings out the worst in us."

"Ruth," broke in Nehemiah, "we debated and settled this question long ago. The sale of nonessential water at premium prices generates essential revenue for our town. If we keep recycling all of these old issues, we shall never get to the new ones. Since it seems you folks have no new business, I suggest we hear the report of our water commissioners."

Jeremiah rose to his feet. His pants were crisply pressed and creased. "Thanks, Nehemiah. As chairman of the water committee, I would like to report on the search for new water wells. As you all know, the searing heat has dried up virtually all surface water; our wells must be dug increasingly deep to tap what remains of the Grafton aquifer. We have spent a fortune hiring fancy hydrologists who have not located any significant new springs. Modern science has failed us. I think it's time we return to the tried and true science of dowsing. Yes, I can hear the skeptics guffawing. But scientific studies of the effectiveness of dowsing show mixed results: controlled experiments have shown that at least some dowsers find water more reliably than mere chance. Anyway, what other options do we have? If we cannot find more water, then turn off the lights and close the door as you leave town."

Amid agitated murmurs, Judith rose to speak: "Jerry, is that the best you commissioners can do? Why don't we just ask Father Joe to pray to the rain gods? Would any of the other commissioners like to speak?"

Jesse then asked to be recognized by the town manager: "Obviously, if dowsing were cheap there would be no reason to bring the proposal to this meeting. So I'm guessing the commissioners have identified a dowser and that he does not come cheap. Even superstition is now expensive."

Nehemiah let Jeremiah speak: "Our committee is unanimous in this recommendation. Yes, we have identified two dowsers who work together, and yes again, they are expensive. But not as expensive as the raft of hydrologists we brought in. The dowsers are twins: Thomas and Thomasina (I kid you not). They are reported to produce excellent results in other towns."

Pastor Melanchthon asked to speak: "So the whole town is being asked to financially support geomancy? Make no mistake: despite its quaint patina of folksiness, dowsing is pagan occultism. Martin Luther himself condemned dowsing in 1518 as a violation of the First Commandment."

Nehemiah thanked the good pastor for his helpful fatwa and asked if any other ministers objected to dowsing.

Brother Zosima asked to be recognized. His voice was barely audible: "Really, Mel, geomancy? When the Israelites were in the desert, Moses discovered springs of water with his staff. How is that occultism?"

At this point, the town manager began to fidget nervously: "OK, before this turns into a holy war, let's agree that anyone who has a religious objection to dowsing will be exempt from financially supporting it."

After some further discussion, the motion to hire the twins passed overwhelmingly.

As the sun came up, the town settled down. With the first rays of light, windows were shuttered, curtains drawn, and doors closed tight. All the bustle of work and commerce ceased as everyone returned home to sleep or at least to rest, sleep being hard to come by in the searing summer heat. With the absence of humidity, there was no gradual misty or foggy transition from night to day: the Sun attacked the whole landscape all at once, its laser-like beams penetrating and incinerating everything visible. We lived in an Edward Hopper world, vulnerable and exposed to the rapacious light. Daylight meant a continual interrogation to the third degree. Winter was the favorite season, when we suffered only oblique assault.

Esther brought her kids home from the playground for their 6 a.m. dinner before bedtime. Esther and her best friend Boaz both worked at the new hospital, where jobs had opened up when the college moved north. But their spouses, Mordechai and Hannah, had moved with the college because the money was so much better. As soon as Esther closed up the house, she was reminded of the subtle stench of the waterless toilets. Luckily, her kids had known nothing different. She cleaned their hands with alcohol and lanolin before dinner. Then after dinner, she read them a bedtime story, "Goodnight Sun." The younger kids soon dozed in their beds, but Jacob, the oldest, stayed up listening to the old Beatles song "Here Comes the Moon." Esther sat down to do some interfacing for her job.

But soon she grew restless. She recalled that her friend Hannah would be back in town to visit her husband Boaz, so she interfaced Hannah and invited them to come over, since it was still only midmorning. Esther poured some wine and waited for the discrete knock on the door. Hannah and Boaz let themselves in and gave Esther a big hug. Esther and Hannah had grown up together in the village: Esther always idolized Hannah for her blonde beauty and athleticism, while Hannah admired Esther for her compassionate heart and good grades. After the exchange of pleasantries, Esther asked Hannah:

"How is Mordechai doing? We interface every day, but I still find it hard to read people long-distance; he always put on a brave face."

"Oh, don't worry about him. He's doing great! I see him every day at the hospital."

"I hope he's not doing too well without me!"

There was an awkward silence.

"How are you doing, Esther, aside from obviously missing Mordechai?"

"You don't want to know."

At this point, Boaz broke in and suggested that they all sit down, drink some wine, and talk things out.

Esther blurted out: "I have had it with this heat; we are prisoners in our homes! I remember my psychology professor in college telling us that heat causes crime. Each degree of rising temperature leads to a predictable rise in crime, especially crimes of passion. I find it increasingly difficult to control my own anger. Yesterday, I slapped Essau in the face. I must be losing it. And the water rations have been increasingly annoying, but when I float the idea of moving north to the kids, they go ballistic. They have known nothing but our desert."

"Gosh, Esther, you must think we're basking in the cool, wet weather up north, but I can tell you that even in that part of the United States called Canada things are heating up rapidly. Some folks at the college are already talking about moving further north, which would mean the Arctic Circle! Remember that the cacti are always greener somewhere else."

Boaz jumped in to support Esther's frustration. "Yes, fifty years ago, when something might have been done to mitigate this global meltdown, many people denied that human activity was responsible for the rising temperatures. We pretend to be appalled when we read that primitive people sacrificed their own children, but what did our parents do if not sacrifice their own children and grandchildren to the Moloch of their own selfish comfort?"

Hannah continued without a pause: "Not to change the subject, but, Esther, when did you decide to become a blonde?"

"I don't recall when I decided . . . but I soon discovered that hair color doesn't matter much when no one can afford to wear long hair anymore. When I see a rich lady with long hair, I just want to attack her with scissors!"

Another awkward silence.

"I love your new shoes."

"No wonder. You're wearing the same style!"

Boaz attempted to short-circuit this escalating rivalry: "Well, let's have a toast. We raise our glasses to celebrate the fact that wine is now cheaper than water."

"I guess Jesus today would have to turn wine into water. Now that really would be a miracle!"

"Seriously, Hannah, what is Mordechai up to these days?"

Hannah looked a little sheepish: "Mordechai misses you and the kids, obviously, but he loses himself in his work. I don't think he ever leaves the hospital. In fact, he often sleeps in an empty patient bed . . . or, at least, that's what he tells me."

Esther suddenly turned to Boaz and put her hand on his arm: "How are you doing, Boaz?"

Boaz nervously withdrew his arm. "Esther, you know perfectly well. We talk at the hospital every day."

Boaz then collected himself and attempted to lighten up the conversation: "Instead of all this dreary time apart and all this arduous travel, wouldn't it be much simpler if Mordechai and I just traded wives? 'Love the one you're with!'"

On a day much anticipated, the twin dowsers Thomas and Thomasina arrived at the town hall just as the sun was setting. They were met by town manager Nehemiah and water commissioner Jeremiah who soon discovered that Thomas and Thomasina were virtually indistinguishable: both were of medium height and slender build. With her sandy-colored hair cut short, Thomasina could easily pass for a man. Both

Nehemiah and Jeremiah attempted to make eye contact with the twins, but they soon noticed something strange: both twins had a wandering eye. As they stood side by side, Thomas's right eye and Thomasina's left eye migrated to opposite walls, meaning that each made eye contact with their hosts with only one eye. This created the disturbing impression that in talking to them, one was actually seeing eye to eye with only one person.

Thomasina sensed the distress of her hosts and offered: "Alright, I know how disfiguring our vision impairment can seem, but I can promise you that it does not affect our work. No one ever supposed that dowsing was based on vision. In fact, we are convinced that our vision impairments have given us greater sensory awareness in our other modalities."

Nehemiah and Jeremiah stopped staring and promptly apologized.

Thomasina continued: "I know that Thomas does not agree with me, but I believe that dowsing requires a peculiar sensitivity to the pull of the magnetic north pole, as with compasses. Iron particles ionize the water so that it has a magnetic field. Dowsing has always been most successful in areas with high iron content in the water."

Thomas broke in: "Maybe. In my view, traditional arts like dowsing, acupuncture, chiropractic, and so forth are often effective in practice even though their practitioners have no solid theory for how they work. Practice is not merely applied theory; practice has its own logic and history. We don't need a scientific theory to explain how we find water. We just find it."

Jeremiah decided to cut to the chase: "What happens if you find water on private land?"

Thomas replied: "In the Western states, groundwater is generally publicly owned, but here in the East, groundwater is usually privately owned. Therefore, we will begin by searching on public lands."

Thomasina added: "Yes, I have read what can happen when a new water source is discovered on private land and the owner attempts to sell it for profit."

"Indeed," said Nehemiah, "that is precisely what we hope

to avoid here. So I am hereby providing you with a land use map of our village. Use it to limit your search to public and conservation lands."

"Since we must work at night, it can sometimes be tricky to follow boundary markings, but we shall do our best. Even if we cannot see too well, we hear you!"

"Perhaps one of us could accompany you on your search," Jeremiah offered.

"No, as you'll see in our contract, we only work alone."

As they left the meeting, Nehemiah said to Jeremiah: "Those twins give me the creeps."

Although everyone in our village was issued water sufficient for drinking and some cooking, many people used their drinking rations for bathing and household cleaning. After all, in this Puritan culture "cleanliness is next to Godliness," and bathing often took priority over adequate hydration. Only a few people experienced delirium or severe fever, but many suffered from fatigue, headaches, and shriveled skin. Hospitals reported rising rates of urinary-tract infections and kidney stones. Pervasive discomfort turned our town into an emotional tinderbox.

A special town meeting was called to discuss the discovery of a new water source by the twins. It took Nehemiah longer than usual to bring the meeting to order.

"Folks," he said, "listen up. Just like in the old Borscht-belt jokes, I have good news and bad news. The good news is that after weeks of fruitless searching, the dowser twins have finally discovered a significant new location where we can tap the Grafton aquifer. The bad news is that this new well seems to be located on private land, and the owner expects to be compensated for the use of this new well."

Naomi jumped in: "I thought we agreed to search only on public lands precisely to avoid a nasty conflict over water rights?"

"Indeed," replied Nehemiah, "but we discovered a discrepancy between our town survey maps and the deed of the property in question. We have consulted a prominent land-use attorney who says that the description in the deed combined with the granite property markers supersedes the town survey. The owner of the property knows that our current water reserves are low, so he expects to reap a sizeable royalty for access to the new well."

Naomi raised her hand: "I'd like to hear from the water commissioner and from the town selectmen. What are our options?"

"I'll take that as my cue," said Jeremiah. "In addition to consulting with the land-use attorney, we consulted with the dowsers, since they have had experience with such conflicts. I'll let them speak for themselves."

The twins rose together and approached the podium. There was an audible gasp when the townspeople got a good look at them. "In New England, with its tradition of riparian water rights, we have learned to search only on public or conservation lands. But, as we have discovered here, town survey maps are not always accurate. Property owners have a much stronger incentive than do public officials to know the exact boundaries of their holdings. As a result, deeds are much more precise than land-use maps. So yes, we have had some experience discovering water on what turned out to be private property. I wish I could be more upbeat about the prospects for a happy outcome. We have seen towns attempt to take the land without compensation under 'eminent domain'; this always leads to years of litigation, by which time the well might become dry. We have also seen towns attempt to persuade, cajole, bribe, and threaten owners into selling for cheap, but this rarely works. The property owner has the town over a barrel. Unfortunately, these conflicts create horrible divisions in towns, often leading to actual violence, which is why we have not released the name of the property owner."

Ahab interjected suddenly: "I want to hire a dowser to look for water on my property; why should that son of a bitch be the only one to get rich?" Several other voices endorsed this idea.

All eyes turned to the twins, who replied: "No responsible dowser would step into such a volatile situation; it would be throwing gasoline on a fire. But I don't doubt that you could find some quack to take your money."

Someone in the back of the room shouted: "Let's find the new well and just take it from the owner." Many grumbled in assent; some protested.

Nehemiah pounded his gavel on the podium and said: "Until we have a plan for the acquisition of the new water, no one will know where it was found or who owns it. So let's come up with a plan."

Ahab said: "Back to my idea: if we found enough water on other properties, then we would not need this new well."

Jeremiah jumped in: "Almost all existing properties already have wells, and property owners have long had a strong financial incentive to find water. So we figure that only the largest properties would be likely to contain new, undiscovered water supplies."

Nehemiah blanched and pulled Jeremiah aside, saying to him privately: "Jerry, please shut up. You practically identified the owner of the new well."

Nehemiah again pounded his gavel and said: "Look folks, bottom line, we are going to have to pay for this new water. Let's figure out how to raise the revenue."

Naomi jumped in: "So we're back to 'soak the rich' again. How about a new idea for a change?"

Sarcastic voices from the back erupted: "Should we screw the middle class instead?"

Nehemiah turned to Reverend Luke, who said: "Scripture tells us: 'To those whom more is given, more is expected.' The rich among us ought to do their fair share."

But Pastor Melanchthon, in a moment of Christian charity, offered: "Luke, Scripture also says that 'To those who have much, more will be given; and to those who have little, what little they have will be taken from them.' So let's try to refrain from stirring up envy. Let's hear from Father Joe."

I rarely spoke at, or even attended, town meetings, but I stood up. "With all due respect to my brothers in faith, I don't think we are going to find the answer to this quandary in the Bible. We Catholics believe natural justice means that the claims of private property must be limited by the requirements of the common good. What this means is that there is a social mortgage on all private property. The water rights of the new well already belong to the town as a whole. If I knew who the owner was, I am sure I could convince him."

Pastor Melanchthon urgently signaled the desire to speak, so Nehemiah reluctantly recognized him: "Joe, your rosy and naïve view of human nature never fails to amaze me. Do you really think that Aristotle and Aquinas are even remotely a match for human sin? We have already been told that this well owner is determined to enrich himself. What chance do your arguments have against the power of Mammon? Realistically, our options are either to simply expropriate the water by force or to pay off the owner."

The room erupted with protests, angry murmurs, and inarticulate expressions of frustration. Nehemiah decided to adjourn the meeting.

Naomi was sitting down to her evening breakfast when a rock crashed through her kitchen window. When she recovered from the shock, she picked up the rock and noticed the glistening quartzite ribbon running through it. The rock was painted with the letters "WB," which stood for the infamous Water Brigade, a shadowy gang of vigilantes determined to get the owner of the new water rights to yield them to the town. Naomi, like other large landowners in the town, had already endured other acts of vandalism and graffiti, so this new outrage was not unexpected. Over time, the definition of the hated "kulaks" came to include almost everyone who owned a lot larger than a half acre. The police began arresting minor offenders, and the local jails were soon full.

Naomi's husband, Ahab, did not have the patience of Job. He and some other large landowners began a series of reprisals against random condo communities and trailer parks. Their motto was: "Threat for threat, rock for rock." Indeed, those citizens with the strongest reputations for moral uprightness were also most insistent upon the need for just retribution. Morality became an ally of revenge; justice colluded with retaliation. Everyone believed that he had been attacked first; everyone exonerated himself on the grounds that unjust aggression had to be met with just punishment. There was no Leviathan to step in and say: "I don't care who started it; you are both grounded."

The escalating violence alarmed many citizens, and the churches began organizing prayer vigils to enlist the help of the Prince of Peace. But the attacks and counterattacks expanded to include hundreds of families. Many people began to realize that the moral distinctions between aggressor and victim no longer made any sense: almost everyone had become both a victim and an aggressor. Instead of people making use of violence, it seemed as if the violence was making use of them, for its own purposes.

Nehemiah and the selectmen realized that the fear and hatred gripping the town must be addressed directly in a town meeting. Weapons scanners were set up around the entrances to the gymnasium. Townspeople filed into the gym in tense silence. There was very little banter or even eye contact. Everyone looked at his or her neighbors warily.

Nehemiah addressed the assembled citizens: "Folks, we need to talk about our water resources and how to step back from the brink of madness. The only way I can see out of this destructive cycle of violence is to declare a general amnesty: No one will be prosecuted for recent attacks on property so long as he accuses no one else of wrongdoing."

Many angry protests were murmured. Then I spoke: "Maintaining the moral order requires us to distinguish the innocent from the guilty, the victim from the aggressor. I do not see the justice in ignoring these fundamental moral distinctions. Therefore, I oppose the amnesty."

Brother Zosima slowly approached the podium: "Joe, can't you see that what you call morality is just another form of violence? What could be more aggressive than condemning another human being? Only God can judge. Innocent or guilty? Who among us is either truly innocent or fully guilty? So long as we insist on morality, justice, and our rights, we shall all perish. Instead of attempting to assign blame, we must accept that each of us is responsible for what everyone else does."

Pastor Melanchthon asked to speak: "I agree with the good Zosima that it is dangerous for us to attempt to usurp God's final judgment. I also agree that each of us is both saint and sinner, so we must be careful of moral righteousness. But that is why God appoints civil authorities to uphold the sword of justice in this sinful world. So let's take a vote on this amnesty proposal."

Brother Zosima continued: "Our choice today is not between just violence and unjust violence; it is between nonviolence and nonexistence. The way of the Gospel is remote from any moralizing violence. Either we are radically converted to the Gospel of peace or we face uncontrollable and apocalyptic violence. We must support this amnesty so that the real work of conversion might begin."

The assembled citizens began to bicker and argue chaotically about the proposed amnesty. Nehemiah was struggling to maintain order in the room. Then the police chief burst into the room, accompanied by the town assessor. The chief mounted the podium: "Folks, I am very sorry to have to tell you this, but Joshua was murdered in his home last night. We don't have a suspect, but we do have a motive. The town assessor has confirmed that Joshua was the landowner on whose land the new water well was discovered."

Many angry and distressed comments arose from the room, ranging from "Serves him right" to "We are all guilty."

Nehemiah addressed the meeting: "If ever the irrationality of violence were doubted, consider this: we have no access to these water supplies until his estate is finally settled in probate court, which could take years. So we now face a town riven with hatred and violence and no new water resources."

Despair began to register on the faces of the townsfolk as they realized that all this bitter and destructive conflict had led them nowhere. Several people murmured to the effect that their town would have been better off had the twins never arrived. Each person in the room began to look for the dowser twins, and soon the crowd began to separate into two unequal parts: the twins and the rest.

The eye is faster than the tongue. Even before anyone could yell, "Grab the twins," all eyes landed upon them. If looks could kill! Soon they were "escorted" up to the podium. Their disfigured eyes now looked not just bizarre but monstrous, repelling any hint of sympathy that might have come their way.

Nehemiah broke the tense silence and announced that the meeting would be adjourned so that an investigation regarding the murder of Joshua could commence. Meanwhile, Thomas and Thomasina would be held in protective custody for their own safety. Suddenly the power failed, and the room went pitch dark. Amid confusion, shouts of panic, and sounds of a scuffle, the power was soon restored. With light came comfort and calm, as each citizen silently exited the gymnasium, but not without first drinking in the sight of the two corpses laid out as in a wake. Not a word was spoken as the townsfolk looked upon what they had wrought, and they left the gym with the dignity and solemnity of a congregation exiting a Good Friday service.

Over the next week, members of the Water Brigade began to post public apologies for their deeds; then, wealthy village residents began to share their surplus water supplies. A new tone of civility was manifest in letters to the editor, in messages to the town crier, and in casual barbershop conversations. All who attended the November 5th emergency town meeting seemed shell-shocked by what they had learned about their own capacity for hatred and violence. Now folks treated each other with kid gloves and with a courtesy that was unprecedented. Some cynics grumbled: "I wonder how long this will last?" But others were wondering how to routinize or institutionalize this pervasive feeling of solidarity.

The town selectmen decided to schedule all future town meetings on the fifth day of the month to honor that tragic November day. On December 5th, the town met in a spirit of harmony to pass a general amnesty and to pool all water resources. The informal sharing of water over the past month had proven to everyone that there was plenty of water in town once the hoarding ceased. The shortages were the result of mutual suspicion more than of natural drought. As the water commissioner put it: "We can either drink together or be thirsty alone." Many citizens wondered why they had not been able to come together until the tragic violence of November 5th.

Nehemiah stunned the assembled citizens with his proposal that Thomas and Thomasina be honored with a memorial plaque in the town hall. At first, the genial spirit of harmony in the room began to fray.

Naomi burst out in anger: "What? Honor the people who brought a plague of violence to our village?"

But Jeremiah reminded her that she had not been present at the fateful emergency meeting in November: "All we do know is that they managed, at a fatal cost to themselves, to save this town. Even if new water resources had become available on Joshua's property, the well of our village's civic trust had been poisoned by mistrust, causing dangerous hoarding of precious water. What we have discovered since that fateful day is that our enemy was not Joshua or the dowser twins but our own selfish rivalries and mutual suspicion. We owe this discovery to the sacrifice of Thomas and Thomasina. I think they deserve to be honored."

The room fell into a reflective silence, which seemed to signal consent. So Nehemiah called the question, and the proposal to honor the twins was approved unanimously. In addition to the plaque in the town hall, the graves of Thomas and Thomasina are now commemorated with fresh flowers each week.

A month later, an anonymous donor paid to have their dowsing rod bronzed; it now hangs on the wall of the gymnasium near the exit. The bronze is especially shiny where everyone touches the rod on their way out of town meetings. Stranger still, we now begin each town meeting in silence as we all take a drink from one large goblet of municipal water. The goblet is inscribed with the names of the twins and these words: "Each of us is responsible for everyone else."

CHAPTER TWO

Why Do We Read Literature? A Symposium

Cole Porter: Ladies and Gentlemen, welcome to Yale. My name is Cole Porter, class of 1913, and I shall be your symposiarch. As the center of academic literary criticism in the twentieth century, from the New Critics to Deconstruction and beyond, my alma mater seems like the ideal venue for a symposium on the question of why we read literature. Our special guest this evening is the French literary theorist, anthropologist, and theologian René Girard, who has just been elected to the Académie Française. René, you're the top! We are meeting in Berkeley College, appropriately named for a great philosopher. Our college *cave à vin* has a splendid collection of fine wines, which we shall be sampling. Wine leads us to truth, which is evident in Yale's motto: *in vino veritas*. I cannot provide the dancing girls of Plato's *Symposium*, but I shall on occasion annoy you with some music on the piano.

Socrates: As you all know, I have some familiarity with symposia. And although I enjoy your humor, Cole, I question your role here. In my day, we would never appoint a mere singer as symposiarch. What on earth could Mr. Porter contribute to our discussion of literature?

Cole Porter: Oh, son of Sophroniscus, sometimes I just don't see what Alcibiades saw in you. Let us commence the discussion. In the words of the immortal poet: "Brush up your Shakespeare, start quoting him now; Brush up your Shakespeare, and the women you will wow." That, in a nutshell, is my theory of literature—a mating song deployed by the male of the species to win over females or, in my case, males too. Yes, every poem aspires to be sung. After all, every word we use to describe poetry derives from songs: lyric, sonnet, lay, hymn, canto, rhyme, ballade, ode, rune, canticle, and psalm.

Oscar Wilde (interrupting): Oh, Colie, you are divine. Your shepherds warble their lays only to get laid. But perhaps I shock my dear friend, the Red Virgin—or should I call you "La Pucelle"?

Simone Weil: If only I had the strength of Joan of Arc! Oscar, flattery will get you nowhere—except, perhaps, to Heaven.

Cole Porter: Yes, Oscar, we poets are the nightingales of our species. Why do we sing? Let me answer with another rhetorical question. Were any of the great poets chaste? Apart from dear Plato, who is always a special case, I think not. Who can resist a poet? Remember Tom Stoppard's *Shakespeare in Love?* Young Will recites his lyrics while Gwyneth Paltrow undresses. As for Wordsworth, Shelley, Keats, and Byron, they were not called "Romantic poets" for nothing. So all literature is a mating call, a swoon song designed for no other purpose than to propagate the species. The expression "love poetry" is a pleonasm: all poetry is a love song. Poetry is like a sacrament: it is both a sign and an instrument of invisible love. As I recall, René, you once espoused a theory quite like this?

René Girard (blushing): Cole, thanks for the warm introduction, but perhaps what happens in Paris should stay in Paris. What I most like about Cole's theory is that it is evolutionary, even Darwinian: poetry and song begin in male displays and mating rituals, hence contributing to reproductive success. Truly, birds do it, bees do it, even overeducated troubadours, minstrels, and poets do it. As we know from Don Quixote and Madame Bovary, literature can cause us to fall in love, sometimes disastrously so! If I might generalize your insight, I think we love to read literature and see drama and hear poetry recited because we sense that writers reveal the truth about the human condition, a truth that is ignored or even actively hidden by our philosophers and social science theorists. Ultimately, we seek—and I believe we find—the effectual truth of things more in great literary works than in the works of philosophers and social scientists. Who are the greatest students of human psychology and human social life? I nominate Sophocles, the author of the Gospel of John, Cervantes, Shakespeare, Stendhal, Dostoevsky, and Proust. It has become fashionable, especially in the twentieth century, to turn to philosophers or scientists in order to understand literature: critics read Aristotle, Nietzsche, Freud, Marx, Heidegger, Derrida, Lévi-Strauss, and Levinas in order to illuminate the works of Sophocles, Shakespeare, Dostoevsky, and many others. The assumption behind this widespread practice of criticism is that philosophy and science give us the royal road to knowledge and, thus, can be used to explain what is only inchoately grasped by literary artists. On this view, Freud gave us the scientific theory of the mechanisms of incest and parricide, which we can then deploy to explain family conflict in Sophocles and Shakespeare. And Marx gave us theories of class conflict, which we can use to explain social conflict in works from Jane Austen to James Joyce. But is it true that Freud or Marx is a better guide to the truth of the human condition than is Sophocles or Shakespeare? We have been so busy teaching grey theory to our great imaginative writers that we have forgotten what we might learn from them. After all, is it not plausible to argue that Sophocles understood oedipal conflict before reading Freud? Or that Balzac and Zola understood class conflict without having to read Marx?

Oscar Wilde (interrupting): Bravo, René! Theoreticians are just bad literary artists: those who can, write; those who cannot, theorize. Everything Marx knew about nineteenth-century class conflict was invented by Balzac.

René Girard: Now, obviously, Freud and Marx developed elaborate and quasi- or perhaps pseudo-scientific theories of family conflict and of class conflict. But, I ask you, how well have those ideas aged with time? We still read Sophocles and Balzac avidly, but who today still reads Freud or Marx?

Simone Weil: In deference to the prejudices of our demotic age, Girard fails to mention that all his literary masters are geniuses. Yes, great literature, works of genius, do provide a unique window on reality. Great literature brings us closer to actual life than does even the best theory because of its density, its specific gravity. Theorizing is always abstract and sees the world at a great distance, in which all colors fade to grey. From an airplane we see a lot but nothing looks real. Lived reality is vivid and sensuous; it can be captured only by the richer palette of literary art. However, great literature is not only more real than scientific theories, but it is also more real than our own lives. What is human life, alas, other than fantasies about the future and sentimental fictions about the past? Our lives are little more than the stuff dreams are made of—to coin a phrase. Looking forward, our self-dramatizing narcissism leads us to imagine either fantastic glories or disasters for ourselves; looking backward, we shamelessly rewrite our own memories to flatter our egos. The only thing real about us is our capacity for self-delusion. Most "literature," meaning romantic and heroic pulp-fiction, simply reinforces these satanic illusions. But a few works of great literature shatter the fictions we live by and offer us glimpses of reality.

René Girard: Our lives are fictitious, and only our great novels are real. But as T. S. Eliot said, human beings can only bear reality in small doses.

Oscar Wilde: I must object to this unwarranted assumption that we ought to prefer reality to illusion. Only fake people search for reality; real people prefer to dream. Reality is the nightmare from which art awakens us. Let Eliot have his reality medicine each day. I prefer to sup on splendid illusion.

Socrates: As someone who never wrote anything, I resent all this talk about books! I wonder whether genuine knowledge can be found in books of any kind, literary or theoretical. I prefer the movement of living thought in the adventure of conversation. Girard asks rhetorically, "Who reads Freud or Marx anymore?" Read Freud or Marx? Heavens no! All that heavy Teutonic science is dreadful. But I have spent some wonderful long evenings talking with them in London: Freud is no strict Freudian nor is Marx a Marxist, after a few beers. Once thought is pinned down, like a butterfly in a specimen book, it has long been dead. We murder to dissertate. Indeed, it is widely known that René's ideas are conveyed much better in long interviews than in his monographs. But I think this is true generally: we'd be much better off with philosophical dialogues than with philosophical treatises. Which would you prefer: Spinoza's geometrical *Ethics* or a dialogue between Spinoza and Leibniz? Reading Hegel's *Encyclopedia* or seeing him debate Kant about the nature of reason? I choose living thought, not dead books.

René Girard: "I hate books," says the most renowned author of the French Enlightenment, Jean-Jacques Rousseau. He is at his best, naturally, in his novel *Julie*, which lays bare the logic of the romantic triangle. So unlike Jean-Jacques, at least you lived by your own creed, Socrates.

Socrates: If I understand you correctly, René, you are arguing that poets have genuine knowledge of the human soul which they then transmit to their listeners. But knowledge is more than a mere sum of true beliefs; knowledge involves the acquisition of true beliefs justified by evidence and logical reasoning. But in my conversations with poets, I see not the slightest hint of an attempt to justify any beliefs: no real evidence, no definitions, no arguments, and no proofs—hence, no knowledge. On the other hand, as with all crafts, poetry is based on some knowledge of what is imitated: the shoemaker must have knowledge of human feet, and the poet must have some knowledge of the human soul in order to reliably produce his effects. Thus, when I talk to craftsmen, they can tell me what they are trying to produce and why. But when I spoke to the poet Ion, as you may recall, he could provide no rational account of his poetry; he could only wax lyrical about the inspiration of the Muses. Insofar as poetry is a kind of rhetorical craft, then there is some knowledge involved (at least knowledge of how to produce effects, not necessarily knowledge of the soul itself); but insofar as poetry is a fine art, then there is no knowledge at all, only oracular pronouncements. When you treat literature purely as a source of scientific knowledge, then you have no theory of literature per se, just a theory of science.

René Girard: You may be right Socrates. Like many French café intellectuals, I am a better talker than I am a writer. And you are also right that I have no interest in the genres of writing. I believe that Lévi-Strauss and Cervantes are both anthropologists, and if you were to ask me, we have more to learn from Cervantes. What do we learn? Thanks for asking! In my first book, I contrast the Romantic lie with the truth found in novels. The Romantic lie is the modern delusion that each individual person is or ought to be the source of his or her own desires. This delusion is central to the whole myth of modern individualism, which asserts that we create ourselves, that we are self-made. Our best novelists have shown us the truth: all desire is social, not individual. We love a particular girl only because we see someone else love her. Without a potential rival, there is no desire for anything. All desire is mimetic. We see this in small children, who will routinely ignore a toy until they see another child play with it. Well, desire in novels is always social, imitative, and rivalrous. Since I regard these views as giving us the foundation of the truth of the human condition, I see poets, dramatists, and novelists as our greatest anthropologists. Moreover, I also regard all major works of literature as autobiographical. Read carefully, every great novel or drama reveals a personal conversion of the author, from naïve illusion to a genuine knowledge of the truth about human beings. Writing is both a cause of this conversion and a representation of it. I see my theory of mimetic desire as a development of Socrates's views of poetry as mimesis in the *Republic*.

Socrates: By the dog, did I hear you say "mimesis?" Actually, I argue that all crafts are mimetic and that poetry is mimetic only to the extent that it is a craft—poetry stemming from divine inspiration is not mimetic. The only real objects are the purely intelligible forms: a craftsman looks to this form in order to make an artifact. The artifact participates, indirectly, in the reality of the form or idea; the artifact is an imitation of the form or idea. Were there not an intelligible idea or form of a table, we could not explain why all craftsmen in all times and places make similar tables. This also explains how craftsmen know in advance what they will make: they grasp the form or idea in thought. The artifact is merely a pale reflection of that intelligible idea. Then the painter or poet depicts that artifact, as Homer depicts Achilles's shield. So, on my account your poets and writers are twice removed from reality and, hence, not very trustworthy.

But recall that poetry is not mere craft; it is also a fine art involving inspiration. This dimension of inspiration explains why creative artists, unlike craftsmen, do not know in advance what they will create. By some mysterious dialogue between craft and divine inspiration, something new emerges. As I discovered from my frustrating conversation with the poet Ion, these creative artists simply can give no account of what they have created. I remember Picasso telling his students: "If you know in advance what you want to create, don't bother!" Art is mimetic only to the extent that it is a craft. The fine arts are a divine—some would say diabolical—blend of mimesis and madness.

Moreover, I understand the relationship between poetry and desire differently from you. I expel the poets from my ideal City in Speech because they have imitated vicious human conduct—rape, adultery, incest, and parricide are their favorite themes. Even worse, the poets depict the gods in the same debased ways: their gods are no better than real men, except that they do not die. And if we want children to imitate the gods, then we need to expose them to a truthful picture of the gods, not these lusty divine marauders. Instead of men imitating virtuous gods, we have our gods imitating vicious men. I don't think children are in danger of imitating the desires of the gods, whatever those might be; the danger is when children want to imitate the deeds of the gods. I will readmit the poets to my city when they agree to represent the gods accurately and to record the deeds only of virtuous men.

Aristotle: Actually, Socrates, René's theory of mimesis is closer to mine than to yours. After all, René's claim is not so much that art is mimetic but that human beings are essentially mimetic. According to him, we acquire all of our desires within a social context of imitating the desires of others. The great novelists, he says, have merely reported this fundamental truth about human beings. As he has noted in some of his interviews, I wrote in my *Poetics* that man is the most imitative of all animals and that art arises from this primordial instinct to imitate. Surely this insight is the basis of René's work.

René Girard: Dante was right that you are "the master of those who know." Yes, my aim, like yours, is a philosophical anthropology, not a mere poetics. But poetics leads us to anthropology, and I note that your deepest insight into human nature came not in your *Ethics* or *Politics* but in your *Poetics*. With the recent discovery of mirror neurons, today's neuroscientists have proven that mimesis is at the core of human cognition. So modern science has confirmed that "man is the most imitative of all animals." Still, I find your discussion of social mimesis to be naïve because you don't point to the destructive rivalry and violence generated by mimesis. You see only a virtuous circle of friends imitating each other's goodness.

Aristotle: René, unlike you, I do believe in the importance of genre (that is, of genus and species), so I will respectfully refuse your invitation to theorize human nature here, and I will stick to the principles of poetics. I hesitate to criticize Socrates because I am his friend, but I am a greater friend of the truth. I think we must distinguish the material, formal, efficient, and final causes of a drama or epic poem. It cannot be the case, as Socrates claims, that the real work of art is the merely intelligible archetype. Every work of art is an artifact and must have a material instantiation. There is no such thing as purely "conceptual" art. Without a material substrate there is no artifact, and every work of art, no matter how creative, is also an artifact. The formal cause of the work is the conceptual shape given the matter by the craft and inspiration of the artist. Here is the purely intelligible form that Socrates is so fond of. But the form has its origin not in any heaven of ideas, but in nature. Hence, the formal cause of any work of art is found in nature because all art is an imitation of nature, a doctrine that Socrates also misunderstands, as we shall see later. Poems and dramas are imitations of human actions, and human actions stem, ultimately, from human nature—yes, through the medium of social conventions. Greek drama makes use of different social conventions from, say, Japanese drama, but the familiar family, class, and national conflicts are driven by the same human passions. The efficient cause of a work of art is the motion of the artist, guided by the skill of her craft and also perhaps by divine inspiration. The final cause or purpose of a work of poetic art is the purgation of the soul of the member of the audience from the harmful effects of pity and fear.

Let's return to mimesis. Here is how a work of art imitates nature. Socrates describes mimesis as a kind of imperfect replica or bad copy of the original, as if art imitates nature by photographing or xeroxing it. But that is not what mimesis means. Art imitates nature in processes, not in products. A human house imitates nature not because it attempts to replicate an animal den or lair but because it builds in the same way as nature builds, with the heaviest materials in the foundation and the lightest materials in the roof. Art similarly imitates the physical and psychic causes of nature; art does not copy nature. Despite being an artifact, a work of poetry is more like a living organism than like one of Socrates's tables or chairs because the unity of a work of poetic art is of a much higher order than the unity of a piece of furniture. What gives an organism its unity? What is the source of life, growth, and motion in an organism? Not only is an organism unified in the sense that all of its parts function well together, but it is also unified over time in the sense that it develops its potential into actuality—it grows. What gives an organism its amazing unity, its development, and its life is the soul. When we mark the difference between what is animate or inanimate, we are pointing to a soul. What is the soul of a drama or an epic poem? What makes the literary work come alive, move, and develop? The plot is the soul of a work of poetic art: by means of a well-crafted plot, a poet is able to bring her creation to life. The plot, like the soul, is what gives all the parts of a poem their unity. Unlike Socrates's favorite examples of a chair or bed or table, a work of literary art is more like an organism: it has a beginning, a middle, and an end. Ideally, everything that happens in a work of literature is already implicit in the opening, just as Homer opens the *Iliad* singing of Achilles's wrath or Tolstoy opens *War and Peace* with a St. Petersburg soirée foreshadowing everything that subsequently happens. A work of literary art imitates nature when it unfolds the way an acorn develops into an oak tree.

Oscar Wilde: Oh please, *mon ami le Stagirite*, will you stop this twaddle about art imitating life when it should be obvious that art is far superior to life? Surely, art is more beautiful than life. What does it say about the culture of modern theorists of literature that they can write whole tomes that never even mention the one essential feature of literary art, namely that it be beautiful? We often associate beauty with the visual arts since beauty is said to be in the eye of the beholder. Yet surely music can be beautiful. And literature is beautiful for the same reasons that music is beautiful—because of the resolution of dissonance that we call harmony. Just as composers create harmonic tension and dissonance in their music so that we can enjoy the beautiful resolution, so literary artists create Sturm und Drang in their stories so that we can enjoy the beautiful denouement. If life were consistently beautiful, we should have no need for art. But let's face it, life is often vulgar, ugly, and brutal; nature is often a stingy bitch. Were it possible, we would craft our lives to have the unity that you so well describe in great works of literature. But whose life has the perfect denouement, the perfect closure of Achilles's or Prince Andrei's? Do we have the luxury to epitomize our lives with a death-bed aphorism? (By the way, I plan to exit this world drinking Moët & Chandon Nectar Impérial Rosé so that I can die as I lived—beyond my means.) Our lives are messy, ungrammatical, ill-mannered, and usually in bad taste; art is noble, harmonious, stylish, and witty. In Utopia—and of what possible use is a map that does not include Utopia—life would be as elevated as art; but in this sorry world, we need to escape into art.

Who really believes that art should imitate nature? When I see a sunset I can only think "second-rate Turner." Who wouldn't prefer Shelley's "Mont Blanc" to the original? Or Van Gogh's *Starry Night* to any real sky? Nature is at best raw material for art. When Boucher was asked what he thought about nature as a subject to paint, he said: "Poor lighting and too much green." We can only wish that nature were as beautiful as a Turner, Monet, or Poussin, or that our conversations were as pithy as Shakespeare or La Rochefoucauld. No, let life imitate art!

As for René's literary dogmatics: oh dear me! If poets and novelists had views about "the human condition," then they would have written essays and treatises *propria voce*. But qua poets and novelists (to speak the language of the schoolmen) writers do not have views. Yes, characters in their works express various views, but confusing these with the views of the writer is just plain silly. Does Shakespeare speak through Polonius or through Hamlet? Does Plato speak through Socrates or through Diotima? (I notice Plato is not here at all; he always was elusive). But surely the author has views? Yes, the implied author might very well express views, but the implied author must never be confounded with the actual writer. Heavens! The author is always merely another character invented by the writer; the author is but a mask, a persona. Perhaps the mask is the man? Or is it masks all the way down? I'll leave these puzzles to deeper thinkers. Poems and novels do not have views; only people have views. What could be more dreadful than writers sincerely expressing their heartfelt views through their novels? That is the very definition of bad writing. If writers were honest, rather than vain, they would all use noms de plume so that no one would confuse the author with the writer. René, you are a cultured man; only barbarians search for truth in literature. Enjoy the play of ideas and suspend the barbarism of belief for just one moment.

Immanuel Kant: I'd like to make the case for cognitive values in literature, though perhaps on different grounds from those of Girard (sorry, in Prussia we don't use first names, not even within marriages). Although he claims to eschew notions of genre, Girard does implicitly make a distinction between mythological deception and novelistic revelation. According to Girard, all myths are distorted truths: on the surface they are false but when we decode them we discover a latent truth. Many myths and legends, says Girard, hide the reality of sacrifice and scapegoating in order to sanitize the origin of social order. So, for example, the myth of Romulus and Remus takes the surface form of simple fratricide, but Girard argues that once we demystify the story, we see that actually the whole community ganged up on Remus and killed him as a scapegoat. So Girard thus asserts that Rome was founded not on simple fratricide but, like all communities, on the unity of a lynch mob. He also gives a similar reading of the story of Cain and Abel: Cain, the founder of the first biblical city, is scapegoated by the whole human race by means of "the mark of Cain." On his account, all mythmakers are deceivers: they know the awful truth of scapegoat murder (though they may sincerely believe the victim is guilty), but they hide the all-against-one logic of the foundational murder. By contrast to all myths, which are by his definition deceptive until demystified, the truth, says Girard, can be found in the Gospels and in great works of literature. So he erects a wall between the false genres of myth and religion on the one side and the true genres of the Gospels (sometimes the entire Bible) and great literature on the other. I must say, however, that I do not see this truth-telling contrast: if there are cognitive values to be found in literary works, then they must be present in all genres of literature.

According to Girard, behind every myth is a true historical event that has been bowdlerized to hide the awful truth. But I see no evidence for either of these claims: it is arbitrary and unjustified to presume that all myths, legends, rumors of Jewish conspiracies, and so on, stem from actual historical events. Girard believes that the violence contained in myths truly stems from actual violence, refracted through a distorted lens. For him, where there is smoke, there must be fire. Yet from a naïve reading, nothing seems more like pure fantasy and imagination than a myth: what is a poet, after all, but someone who can generate smoke without any real fire? Where there is smoke, there might be dry ice. But even granting *arguendo* that all myths originate in some actual violent episode, why would the mythmaker distort the nature of that violence? According to Girard, myths are created by the scapegoaters, by the victorious members of a lynch mob to celebrate the origins of their society. Certainly, we can imagine why such a mob would want to deny that the victim was innocent, but why hide the all-against-one logic of the murder? Why not celebrate the triumph of the good community over the sinister individual? Don't we do this frequently in our rituals of capital punishment? Perhaps most myths are merely fantasies. Don't poets just make stuff up? There are just too many plausible alternatives to Girard's reading of myths.

Girard is similarly dogmatic about certain kinds of historical accusations. When he reads medieval accusations that
Jews or witches caused the Plague or poisoned wells, he is
absolutely certain that these accusations led to actual scapegoat murders. Again, where there is smoke (accusations) there
must be fire (real persecution). But not every lurid or fantastic
slander about Jews or witches is prelude to a pogrom, nor is
every pogrom preceded by accusations. Only careful empirical investigation can settle these questions of causation. By
contrast to myths, says Girard, there are the Gospels and
certain great literary works; these genres are by definition
revelatory of truth. Let us focus on novels. Many novels depict,
says Girard, romantic triangles, and this reveals to us the truth
about the nature of mimetic desire. What a leap of logic! Even
a real-life anecdote about a triangle would be very weak
evidence for the centrality of triangles in real human life—but
a *literary* anecdote? Obviously, we do not base our belief in the
existence of love triangles on what we read in novels; rather,
we find them plausible in novels because we are acquainted
with them in real life. Contrary to Wilde, we don't believe that
people form romantic triangles in order to imitate novels!
Rather, we assume that novels imitate life. But if novels are
derivative of real life, then how can novelistic devices, such as
a triangle, constitute evidence of anything real? Compared to
real-life triangles, they are mere hearsay.

Sigmund Freud: I hesitate to accuse Herr Doktor Professor
Kant of faulty logic, but he poses a false dilemma here. The
content of myths and legends is neither literally true nor
simply made up. Take the Oedipus myth, for example. I never
argued that this story is part of the historical record—how
absurd! But neither was this archetypal legend the product of
arbitrary invention. The Oedipus myth is psychically true,
whatever its literal truth. Certain myths resonate with human
nature so profoundly that they cannot *not* be true. That is why
Girard and I distinguish the manifest from the latent content:
a myth might be manifestly false but embody a latent truth.
Although Girard sometimes claims that the myths and legends
he "demystifies" do record, in a distorted way, actual crimes,
I argue that Girard's myths are literally false but psychically

true. Even the horrible libelous rumors about Jews poisoning wells and other crimes cannot be simply ignored because of their absurdity. They reveal deep, though unwelcome, truths about the human need to find scapegoats. To take a more recent example, the accusations against Captain Dreyfus were, of course, historically false; but nothing has revealed more truth about the French psyche.

Where I part from Girard is by rejecting the notion that the latent content of a myth must have some indirect basis in reality. During my neurological practice in Vienna, many of my patients told me of their dreams or even "memories" about sexual relations with their parents. At first, I believed that these fantasies or memories must have some basis in reality, however indirect. I shuddered in horror at the thought of so much incest and abuse in respectable bourgeois homes. But, over time, hearing so many dreams about incest, I began to doubt that common fantasies have any basis in reality. So now the question is: What do fantasies of incest tell us about our psychic needs and conflicts? Our dreams and other fantasies certainly reveal truths, but only psychological truths. I suspect that the same is true about Girard's myths: instead of indirectly revealing historical truths about scapegoat murder, they reveal the psychic need for killing scapegoats. I would say the same thing about French triangles in novels. I doubt there are many such triangles in reality, but boy, we sure love to fantasize about them.

René Girard: Sigmund, you should not have discounted the possibility that your patients were conveying literal truths about childhood incest and abuse. Today, you would be required to report those stories of incest to the police. Perhaps you simply could not face the awful reality of widespread sexual abuse of children, even in "respectable" homes. Do we find a bowdlerized portrait of Viennese family life in your case histories? I refuse to turn away from the awful truth of human violence, which is not primarily a psychic phenomenon. If our myths and legends are full of murder and scapegoating, then so is human life.

Oscar Wilde: It is amusing to hear the sage of Königsberg discuss the cognitive value of novels since he has blamed novels for causing what he calls "the imbecility of women" (and scholars wonder why he remains a bachelor!). I just cannot help but observe how ludicrous it is to look for knowledge in literature. Jerome Stolnitz has effectively demolished such claims by showing how trivial are the alleged "truths" discovered in literature, such as "pride goeth before a fall" or "hubris may destroy a great man." They are almost always banal nostrums or mere bromides. Or consider two famous novelistic "truths": "It is a truth universally acknowledged, that a single man in possession of a good fortune must be in want of a wife" and "All happy families are alike; each unhappy family is unhappy in its own way." Setting aside the irony evident in these pronouncements, what is their cognitive value? Even assuming their truth, a novel by definition can provide no evidence for them. If we affirm them, it can only be on the evidence afforded by real life. Novels might generate hypotheses, but they cannot provide genuine knowledge.

Immanuel Kant: To the sage of Reading Gaol, I should point out that when I speak of the cognitive value of novels, I have something else in mind. Robert Stecker points out that novels often describe with great accuracy the moral codes, etiquette, and customs of the societies in which their stories are set. So we often do learn real facts about the manners and mores of very different societies, ranging from medieval Norway to a Nantucket whaling ship. I think this is one of the great attractions of novels. Of course, as novels they can make no claims about the truthfulness of those descriptions, but scholars can tell us how accurate they are. More important than these putative facts is what we learn about ourselves from how we react to them. Whether they are true or not, we find ourselves attracted or repelled by these strange moral codes and thereby discover a great deal about our own deepest values. In fact, I know no better way to surface one's own ethical convictions than to try on the morals and manners of various novels and see how they feel. So reading novels is primarily a journey of self-discovery. Some literary scholars have seen novels as counterfactual thought experiments that can deepen our understanding of human psychology and rationality. Lisa Zunshine, for example, argues that in real life we are constantly faced with the challenge of mind reading—that is, figuring out what other people are thinking. Of course, we have no direct access to other people's thoughts, so we attempt to infer them based on gestures, words, and actions. Novels can teach us much about our inchoate theories of mind by showing us characters who make these inferences about other characters, sometimes successfully and sometimes disastrously. Moreover, the "omniscient narrator," who sometimes proves fallible, gives us direct access to the thoughts of some characters, enabling us to test our own hypotheses. Zunshine argues that this fascination with mind reading explains the popularity of the detective novel, since in real life we are all detectives.

Similarly, Paisley Livingston argues that novels help to illuminate theories of practical rationality. In standard theories since Hume, conduct has been thought to be the product of both beliefs and desires. When explaining courses of conduct, some philosophers emphasize desires while others emphasize beliefs. Novelists, with their unique capacity for mind reading, can mix a wide variety of desires and beliefs together in their characters to produce a huge array of conduct, thus testing our intuitions about how desire and belief combine to produce various kinds of actions. Novelists play with a kind of practical reasoning chemistry set, mixing desires and beliefs and then waiting for the explosion. Livingston argues that these novelistic experiments deepen our understanding of practical rationality.

In conclusion, I might note that Zunshine and Livingston are still focused on individual psychology and rationality whereas Girard argues that this individualism reflects a "romantic lie" about the true origin of desires. Girard calls for "intervidual" psychology focused on the social microsetting of the novel: for him, the unit of analysis is not an individual agent or character but a triad of relations between two persons and a mutual object. He sees the novelist not as a mind reader, but as a sociologist who explains human conduct by reference to social settings rather than individual motives. What novels teach us, according to Girard, is that our conduct is the product of a particular social situation, not our own allegedly unique beliefs and desires. Anyone in a triangle will behave in the same way: the rivalry will begin with conflict over a mutual object, but as the conflict escalates, the object fades from view, and we are left with a dyadic duel to the death. According to Girard, these structural dynamics are quite independent of each person's supposedly unique personality. He is certainly right that triangular desire is common in novels and poses some very pointed challenges to our individualist psychology and ethics. And it is important to note that triangles are not limited to novels. More recently, Girard has been reading the work of my contemporary and fellow Prussian, Carl von Clausewitz. Girard finds in Clausewitz a structural analysis of war with the same logic as that of the romantic triangle: two nations come into rivalry because of a desire for the same object, but as the conflict escalates, the political object of the war fades and the conflict escalates into mutually assured destruction. The irrational desire to destroy the rival gradually displaces the rational goal behind going to war. The similarity between the novelistic triangle and Clausewitz's analysis of war is fascinating and reveals the merits of Girard's scientific reading of novels.

Leo Tolstoy: According to Girard, novelists have deep intellectual insights into human nature and psychology. And although this might be true, all of Girard's examples of novelistic truth concern the diagnosis of pathological desire, as in a French triangle. Is disease the best guide to human health? No wonder Girard is so fascinated by the late Dostoevsky, another profound student of human pathology. But surely health is prior to disease just as love is prior to envy and spite. We read literature not to diagnose illness but to be inspired by love.

Novelists are sorry philosophers—just ask the critics of my *War and Peace*! At the time, I thought of myself as a bit of a philosopher of history, but the philosophers sure didn't agree. Anyway, I now realize that philosophy is largely irrelevant to the ethical challenges of human life and to social progress. Men are not moved by philosophical ideas but by love: the same divine love that moves the planets and the stars. Although they are often blamed or credited, the *philosophes* did not cause the French Revolution. They were merely justifying the revolution in sentiments that had already been effected by French novelists and dramatists. Throughout the eighteenth century, French literary artists extended the bonds of sympathy beyond traditional caste boundaries by depicting love affairs between persons of different social classes. Just look at Beaumarchais's comedies of illicit love between nobles and servants. As for Rousseau, his most revolutionary work is not the arid *Social Contract*, but his novel *Julie*, which shows us the power of love, capable of conquering all class boundaries. Once the novelists had breached the walls of class hierarchy, it was easy for the *philosophes* to charge the ramparts. The rights of man had no appeal until the love of man had done its work—the novelists revolutionized sentiments long before the philosophers revolutionized ideas.

The purpose of literature is to extend human sympathy beyond geographical, economic, social, and political boundaries. That is why my novels always depict friendships that cross class, national, and regional barriers. Dostoevsky's first novel, *Poor Folk*, which explores the suffering of ordinary Russians with great sympathy, is without question his best novel; it also marks, as Alexander Herzen rightly says, the beginning of Russian socialism. For similar reasons, the greatest American novel is *Uncle Tom's Cabin*. When President Lincoln met Harriet Beecher Stowe, he famously commented: "So you are the little woman who wrote the book that started this great war!" Clearly, the Great Emancipator agrees with me about the revolutionary power of novels. Any literary work is worthy that creates bonds of love, sympathy, and solidarity among all men. And this explains why Shakespeare is such a bad writer. His dramas invite sympathy only for the nobles and royalty: poor Lear, Caesar, Hamlet, Othello, Desdemona, and Ophelia! In his plays, the servants, guards, and soldiers are either lampooned for comic relief or reduced to mere types; even Falstaff is finally dismissed with contempt in *Henry V*. Shakespeare's drama simply reinforces all the traditional barriers to universal human sympathy. Dickens, by contrast, is a truly great writer, and indeed his novels are widely credited by historians for creating the humanitarian sentiments which led to the great Victorian reforms. Only after the novelists tore down the walls of prejudice and opened the floodgates of sympathy could the reformers come along to remove the debris. Bernard Shaw's socialism is not found in his tedious Fabian tracts but in his drama, as when Eliza Doolittle liberates herself from the bourgeois tyranny of Henry Higgins. What Russia most needs now are more writers like Dickens, Stowe, Beaumarchais, Shaw, and Zola to open the hearts of urban and aristocratic Russians to the real suffering of our peasants and workers; we certainly do not need more intellectuals, agitators, or politicians. We need novels not tracts.

Oscar Wilde: Lev Nikolayevich! Your barbaric Christian moralism has not only corrupted your taste, but, much worse, it has ruined your novels. Just imagine how splendid would be *War and Peace* without the lectures or *Anna Karenina* without the homilies! You can have your Harriet Beecher Stowe and William Jennings Bryan. I'll stick to my beloved Walt Whitman. Lev, you settled for being a saint when you could have aspired to be an artist.

Leo Tolstoy: Oscar, what a *poseur*! Surely you are bored by your own fin-de-siècle decadence shtick? You love playing the immoralist, but those of us who have read *Dorian Gray*, not to mention *De Profundis*, know better. Now, where was I? Oh yes, Wayne Booth has also developed an ethics of fiction based on the idea of a bond of friendship emerging between readers and characters, including the implied author. He does not stress the necessity of universal brotherly love as much as I would, but his approach is compatible with mine. Booth is right that just as we evaluate the moral qualities of our acquaintances when choosing friends, so we evaluate the moral qualities of characters (including implied authors) when befriending novels and plays. We tend to absorb by osmosis the moral qualities of those around us, so it is imperative that we choose our friends carefully, and this applies to our fictional friends as well. Fiction helps us learn how to choose friends wisely, and our fictional friends, as much as our real friends—if not more—can elevate or degrade us. Many of us consciously or unconsciously choose fictional characters as role models, revealing the power of fiction.

And Martha Nussbaum, in a different way, also defends my ethical conception of fiction. Her ethics of fiction is less concerned with general principles, such as brotherly love, and is more concerned with moral particularism, such as how to translate love into the local idiom, with all its subtlety and complexity. She is much fonder of Henry James than I am. According to Nussbaum, what novelists—especially James— do is show us the challenges of bringing moral principles to bear on a specific course of conduct in which gestures, tone of voice, diction, and demeanor are all essential. It is not enough to love our neighbor in general; we must know in every partic- ular how to express that love appropriately. Although many philosophers love mankind in the abstract but loathe indi- vidual men, novelists show us how to love individual men and women in the particular contexts of their social circumstances. This means learning many different languages or registers of social life so that each person can be treated in accordance with his or her own expectations of proper social conduct. In this way, as our friend Aristotle memorably said, "a gentleman never insults anyone unintentionally." How we address an older daughter will be different from how we address the younger, and addressing them alone is different from addressing them in each other's presence. Novels help us to become virtuosos of moral life, highly skilled in speaking the many local dialects of moral concern. Morality has its own etiquette, and novels help us to see the fine grain of moral life, which is almost totally lost in the grey theory of philosophical ethics. Unfortunately, Henry James restricted his moral sympathies to a narrow social elite; that is why I will never consider him a great novelist.

Simone Weil: Lev, you are right that writers of literature have a deep moral responsibility. But you need to ground that responsibility in the metaphysical paradox of good and evil. Nothing is so beautiful and wonderful, nothing is so continu- ally fresh and surprising, or so full of sweet and perpetual ecstasy, as the good. No desert is so dreary, monotonous, and boring as evil. This is the truth about authentic good and evil. With fictional good and evil it is the other way around. Fictional good is boring and flat, while fictional evil is varied and intriguing, attractive, profound, and full of charm. For this reason, John Milton fails monumentally as a writer in *Paradise Lost*. His Satan is utterly fascinating and poetic, while his Jesus is totally flat and prosaic. Satan has all the best lines and attracts all the human sympathy and interest. I can assure you that in real life things are quite the opposite. But we should not be too hard on poor Milton. Virtually no writer of fiction has succeeded in making goodness enticing. Austen's Fanny Price is much less appealing than the naughty Emma. It is a measure of Dostoevsky's genius that he could create characters of profound goodness, such as Prince Lev Nikolayevich Myshkin or Alexei Fyodorovich Karamazov, who are as compelling and surprising as his many demonic characters. Immorality is inseparable from literature, which chiefly consists of the fictional. But it is not only in literature that fiction generates immorality—it does so in life itself. For, as I have already said, the substance of our lives is almost exclusively composed of fiction, and, as in all fiction, evil is attractive and good is tedious. Contact with a saint might awaken us momentarily to reality, but soon enough we fall back asleep. Literature of genius liberates us from the illusion of our own comforting fictions and gives us, in the guise of fiction, contact with the dense texture of reality, that density which life offers us every day but which we are unable to grasp because we are amusing ourselves with lies. To reproach a writer for immorality is merely to reproach him for lacking genius. It is completely vain to seek a remedy for the immorality of literature. What can be remedied is the usurpation by writers of the office of spiritual guidance, for which they are singularly unsuited. In reality it is only the saints who can perform this office.

Leo Tolstoy: I can tell you from experience, Simone, that it is much easier to create compelling characters who are morally bad than to make moral virtue interesting and attractive. I think C. S. Lewis explains this well in his discussion of why Satan is so much more memorable than Jesus in *Paradise Lost*. To create an evil character a writer has only to look within himself. By unleashing some of our own demonic desires and watching them create imaginary havoc, we have a surefire way to understand evil motivations. How many times a day do we wish someone dead or in our beds? By simply relaxing our own self-censorship for one minute, we unleash monsters by the dozen. But who can imagine the interior life of a saint? Only a saint can understand a saint. Apart from you, Simone, writers have simply no idea what it would feel like to be an angelic person. Hence, they cannot bring one to life in their novels.

Sigmund Freud: Perhaps C. S. Lewis has been reading my theories of self-censorship and the demonic unconscious? As you know, I am also very interested in why we read literature. I'll bet you are expecting me to talk about literature in relation to the family romance and the resolution of neurotic conflict. Yes, the Americans have turned psychoanalysis into an industry, and one branch of that industry is the often crude psychoanalytical readings of literature. Now, obviously, I believe that some literary works do illuminate basic psychological mechanisms, but I do not believe that most people turn to literature for therapeutic reasons. And for good reason: therapy is about talking, while literature is about listening.

Psychoanalysis emphasizes the continuity between the child and the adult. We never escape childhood; the unresolved anxieties of children reappear as the neuroses of adults. But not all sublimation is pathological. Let's consider childhood play: children spend a great deal of their free time engaged in fantasy play. Children not only create extraordinary worlds in their imaginations, but they also live fully in those worlds. Given the evident joy children experience in their fantasy play, it would be awful if adults lost all access to this imaginative world. How do adults recover childhood fantasy play? They daydream. Yet because daydreams are rooted in childhood, adults are ashamed of them. We don't share our daydreams with anyone, not even our spouses. If we happened to be in therapy, we share them only with the analyst. Daydreaming seems childish because it is childish: it reveals the continuity between our childhood and our maturity. What are daydreams about? Ultimately there are only two themes in daydreams: first, Walter Mitty–style heroics and second, romance and the erotic. Of course, these two themes are deeply connected, especially for men: by means of our heroics, we win the females. Now consider the themes characteristic of poetry, drama, and novels. Again, the themes are always heroics and romance. In other words, literary artists have simply articulated their daydreams into art. Literature is a crafty and clever way to daydream; writers are able to artic-ulate their childish fantasy play into lasting works of art. Like children, writers have the ability not merely to erect fantastic worlds but also to move in and enjoy them.

I feel a bit sheepish offering this *homo ludens* theory of liter-ature since we have just been treated to a large menu of high-minded reasons for reading fiction: basically, the quest for the good or the true or the beautiful. But I suspect that all these high motives play a rather minor role in why we read literature. Let's face it: we read fiction in order to enjoy the fantasy play we loved as children. Kendall Walton nicely describes works of literature (as well as paintings, movies, and other representational artifacts) as props in a game of make-believe. Children use household objects, toys, and their parent's clothes as props to stimulate the imagination. A broom is really a witch's ride; a towel is Superman's cape. Well, novels, movies, and paintings are also props which help us to imagine that we are living in archaic Greece or nine-teenth-century St. Petersburg. We make believe that we are getting to know Anna Karenina, and we enjoy pretending to worry about her fate. If we really knew a woman like Anna Karenina, we would not enjoy worrying about her fate, but in our game of make-believe we get to worry about her in a fictional and hence, non-burdensome way. That reading liter-ature is a game of make-believe is thus evident in the emotions we experience. Although we often say that a movie or book is scary, we never actually run for the exit. As Aristotle once observed, fearing fictional fire is very different from fearing real fire. Grieving over the death of a real friend is very different from grieving over the death of a fictional friend. Like children at play, in our fiction we get to travel the world and experience the past, present, and future; we meet the most amazing array of people, animals, and monsters. We imagina-tively experience harrowing adventures, glorious victories, total defeats, illnesses, and even violent deaths without leaving the safety of our homes. Representational art provides an ideal set of props to support elaborate games of make-believe, letting us continue to enjoy the immense fun we had as children.

Immanuel Kant: Tolstoy and I don't agree about much, but I think I can speak safely for both of us when I object in the strongest possible terms to your trivialization of literature. Some of us like to think of ourselves as grownups.

René Girard: Yes, novelistic truth is too important to be compared to a game of make-believe.

Sigmund Freud: The Athenian Stranger in Plato's *Laws* argues that play is the only serious human activity and that play brings us closest to the gods. What a splendid compensation for the burdens of growing up! If you think that my theory trivializes literature, then perhaps you disparage childhood and play. You might need some therapy to discover why you do so.

Simone Weil: I'd like to pick up on Freud's observation that, according to Plato, play is the activity that brings us closest to God. I will pass over the irony that Freud is the only person here to mention literature in relation to God. How does literature bring us closer to God? Let me count the ways. First, inasmuch as literature participates in beauty, it participates in the divine source of beauty. Only beauty is not the means to something else; beauty is the only finality in our world. As such, beauty is a symbol of the divine. Art is an attempt to transport into a limited quantity of matter an image of the infinite beauty of the entire universe. If the attempt succeeds, then it reveals rather than hides the reality of the universe. Every true artist has had a real, direct, and immediate contact with the beauty of the world, a contact that is of the nature of a sacrament. The contemplation of beauty always involves love: the beauty of the world is the order of the world that is loved. The only thing truly beautiful is the universe as a whole. The beauty of the world reflects God's love for the world and our love for natural beauty leads us to the source of that order and that love. Jesus praises the lilies of the field, which surpass in beauty any human artifact, showing that God is the one true artist. As our friend Kant argues, beauty is intelligible only in light of divine purpose. He argues that beauty does not give us knowledge of God. Rather, our response to beauty presupposes the reality of divine intelligence. I'll let Kant explain how the sublime in literature leads us to God, for it seems to me that the experience of the sublime, along with the experience of beauty, is the most universal and natural mode of access we have to the divine.

Immanuel Kant: I am delighted to offer a theology of the experience of the sublime. Miss Weil is right that our experience of beauty involves a love of order and that all order presupposes in some way an intelligible purpose. The order of nature is intelligible only in the light of some divine purpose. But this familiar notion of a divine craftsman looks more like a human projection than an insight into the divine reality. The sublime gives us a more profound experience of the fearful divine reality than does the beautiful. Our experience of beauty leads us to those aspects of the divine that are most pleasing and loveable; our experience of the sublime leads us to those aspects of the divine that are least pleasing and most terrifying. Beauty makes us think that we understand divine purpose; the sublime reminds us that we know little of divine purpose.

From Longinus to Edmund Burke, interest in the sublime, as well as in natural religion in general, waxes whenever conventional religion wanes. The contrasts between the beautiful and the sublime are ably described, though poorly theorized, by Burke. The beautiful is bounded, illuminated, perspicuous, and often miniature; the sublime is infinite, obscure, incomprehensible, and vast. Hence, day is beautiful and night sublime; land is beautiful while the sea is sublime. The sublime is terrible, not only because it is unbounded, but also because it is uncontrollable: bulls are sublime while oxen are not; wolves are sublime, while dogs are not. Whatever acts in conformity to our will cannot be sublime. Beauty seduces us; we are ravished by the sublime. Our experience of the sublime involves the delight we take in danger when we are not actually in danger. We enjoy the terrors of Hell in Dante or in Milton from the safety of our study.

How does the sublime lead us to God? The terrible immensity of the mountain ranges, the galaxies, and the oceans is deeply humbling. We are reminded by the sublime in the most forceful way that man is not the measure of all things. The universe cannot be measured out in coffee spoons. Moreover, the sublime in nature is not subject to human will: we cannot rule the stars or seas. All of this chastens our hubris and prepares us to accept our proper place in the great chain of being. Just as the experience of the sublime humbles us, so it elevates God. It is no accident that in every religion the divine is represented in the garb of the sublime: Jehovah speaks through the storm, the mountain, the earthquake, and the fire; his wrath is both vast and uncontrollable. These dramatic displays of divine power are impressive, but what is most sublime about the biblical God is his incomprehensibility, as when he describes himself as "I am who I am," that is, a being with no name, or when he forbids any images to be made of him. A God with no name and with no visible image is truly terrifying. Our first experience of the sublime, then, involves recognizing our own insignificance in the face of the awful magnificence of nature and of nature's God. The sublime reminds us that we are not God. Yet, I believe that the sublime also reminds us of what is great about man. I experience the sublime when contemplating the starry heavens above and the moral law within. Every human person has the amazing capacity to rightly discern his or her moral duty and to obey that duty in the face of the most terrible temptations and threats. This capacity for radical moral freedom even in the face of powerful natural obstacles is sublime and gives human beings a grandeur denied to our physical powers and even to our intellects. Our capacity to sternly rebuke our own moral failings and to submit to the pain of remorse and punishment—in other words, our humility in the face of the moral law, is itself sublime.

Simone Weil: My dear Immanuel, your analytic of the sublime arises like a poetic oasis from the desert of your philosophical scholasticism. I fear, however, that we have been so focused on the content and substance of literature that we have not even mentioned the act of reading. In what way does reading itself—reading of any kind—lead us to God? Reading is a form of prayer, but only when we are attentive: the faculty of attention, when directed toward God, is the very substance of prayer. In our age of unprecedented distraction, the act of attentive reading is threatened as never before. Not only does the love of God have attention for its substance, but the same goes for our love of our neighbor, which we know is the same love. The capacity to give one's attention to a sufferer is very rare indeed. Attention is the purest and rarest form of generosity. Attention is an emptying: we empty ourselves in order to receive the reality of the person we attend. Learning to attend to our books is a crucial pedagogy for learning to attend to the needs of our neighbor and learning to attend to God. In this way, learning to read properly is an invaluable school for love and prayer.

Aristotle: I cannot help but think that there must be something right about all of these accounts of why we read literature, though none of them is fully adequate. Sigmund, I am sorry that my teacher Plato is not here—although I suspect he might have masterminded this whole symposium. He would have enjoyed your account of literature as a game of make-believe. Even if Sigmund is right that our desire to enjoy imaginative play is the most basic and universal motive for reading literature, it might also be true that we come to love the truths, the moral uplift, and the beauty we find in literature. If I might be permitted a simile inspired by Mr. T. S. Eliot: a burglar will throw a steak to a watchdog to distract him so that the burglar can then go about his work. Well, perhaps literary artists entice and seduce us with an invitation to play, and then while we are happily distracted in Walter Mitty–land, the artist goes about the work of teaching us some truth, inspiring us to do some good, revealing some beauty, and perhaps even leading us unawares to God. After all, if novels advertised themselves as sources of knowledge or of moral uplift, no one would read them. But if we get to travel to medieval Norway and meet some elves and trolls, then perhaps we will accept some intellectual and moral education along the way—indeed, in the best literature we won't even notice that our minds are being illuminated and that our hearts are being raised. Plato thought that ideally the education of youth should take the form of play precisely for the benefits of this indirection. Play makes us more receptive to the gifts of knowledge, goodness, and beauty. Indeed, when Hamlet attempts to teach Claudius a pointed moral lesson, he stages a small drama: "The play's the thing."

CHAPTER THREE

Mimetic Desire: A Conversation with William James

René Girard: What an honor to have the opportunity to discuss philosophical psychology with the great William James. You are the founder of scientific psychology in the United States, the founder of the American philosophy of pragmatism, and the first great student of the psychology of religion. In your classic *Varieties of Religious Experience*, you describe religious melancholia with such poetic intensity that I could not tell who you were describing more: me or yourself. I cannot imagine a scholar better suited to discuss my theory of mimetic desire.

William James: René, the pleasure is mine. In a world of narrow academic hyper-specialization, your work, like mine, transcends disciplinary boundaries. Pure philosophers, such as Charles Sanders Peirce, always considered me to be merely a psychologist, while pure scientific psychologists, such as Hugo Münsterberg, denounced me a mere philosopher. I hate to begin with a quibble, but I must qualify your introduction. Rather than the "founder" of scientific psychology in America, I should be called the "importer" of scientific psychology from Germany. And Peirce is truly the founder of philosophical pragmatism, though he changed the name of his own theory to "pragmaticism" when he saw what a hash I had made of his ideas.

How poetic that we should meet at the Hotel Bellagio in Las Vegas to discuss "mimetic desire." Vegas is the Vatican City of imitation and desire. Indeed, some of your books sound as though they were written here: *Deceit, Desire and the Novel, The*

One by Whom Scandal Comes, not to mention *A Theater of Envy.* Is there a backstory here, René?

Your research touches on so many of my passions, psychological, sociological, and religious. Moreover, as someone deeply inspired by the ideals of Christian pacifism, I am intrigued by your account of the origins of violence in mimetic desire. You argue that violent mimetic rivalry was first tamed in ancient times by bloody religious rituals. Well, I once proposed to channel the destructive energies of violent conflict into peaceful campaigns for social justice—what I called "the moral equivalent of war."

René Girard (laughing): Let's call your "moral equivalent of war" by its acronym, "MEOW!"

William James: Très amusant . . . Are you suggesting that my proposal was naïve? Well, let us see how your proposals for controlling violence fare under scrutiny.

I think this conversational format is the best way to explore your ideas since there is no one definitive presentation of your thought, which has evolved over a span of fifty years. And, like me, you are not always very precise in your written formulations—which makes your thought a target-rich environment for your philosophical critics. I am less interested in your published statements than in your underlying positions; I am more interested in your thought than in your words. I propose that we talk first about desire, and then about mimesis, and finally, about mimetic desire.

René Girard: I am no philosopher, and I fear becoming lost in an abstract logomachy. So I propose to lay out three concrete scenarios in which we see the operation of desire, mimesis, rivalry, and ultimately, violence. First, every parent is familiar with this scene: one child observes another child playing with a toy. Even though this first child has seen the toy before, he has expressed no interest in it. But now, having seen another child enjoy the toy, the first child desires that same toy. Second, every reader of literature is familiar with the French triangle: a man takes a passionate interest in a woman but only after he sees her pursued by another man. Third, every student of war (after Clausewitz) is familiar with this disaster: two nations go to war over a mutually-coveted territory but end up destroying themselves. France and Germany fight over Alsace-Lorraine; Russia and Germany fight over Poland and Ukraine. Although such conflicts begin as the rational pursuit of a political goal by military means, they soon escalate into a totally irrational fight to the death—what is called "mutually-assured destruction."

In each of these scenarios, we see a triangle of two agents and a common object. Those persons deluded by "the Romantic lie"—that each individual is the source of his or her own desires—describe these triangles as a tragic conflict between two agents, both with a desire for the same object. On this view, that two men should love the same woman is an unfortunate coincidence. Bah! As Freud reminds us, there are no coincidences. The great novelists have taught me that the triangle itself is the source of desire. A man desires a woman only because he sees or imagines her desired by another man. Desire is not within us; we are in desire. Desire arises from social situations; social situations do not arise from desire. Desire is a sociological not a psychological phenomenon. Hence, I have called for the development of a new kind of truly social psychology, which I call "intervidual psychology."

William James: Many commentators describe your theory of desire in relation to French structuralism. I find any attempt to explain your theory in relation to French structuralism an example of attempting to define the obscure in terms of what is even more obscure. French structuralism, to the extent that I understand it, begins with Saussure's argument that words have meaning, not in relationship to their putative objects but in relationship to other words. By analogy, you are saying that desire gets its meaning not from its putative objects but from the relationship between agents. On your account, then, Robinson Crusoe has no desires until the arrival of the man Friday.

René Girard: Yes, before the man Friday arrives, Crusoe has only animal needs and appetites. Desires arise solely from potential or actual social rivalry. True, animals also have social rivalries, conflicts, and hierarchies, but these are rooted in and limited by biological instincts. Animals fight over territory and over females, but these fights are typically ritualized in

displays of aggression and then settled by rituals of domina-
tion and submission well before mutual destruction.
Compared to human violence, conflicts among animals of the
same species are purely theatrical. Human desire, by contrast,
because it is not rooted in natural instincts, is boundless and,
hence, extremely dangerous. Instead of ritual head-butting,
humans prefer deadly duels. No species other than man is in
danger of total self-destruction.

William James: Most of us associate social life with cooper-
ation, mutual aid, and love, but social life for you means
rivalry, envy, spite, jealousy, and violence.

René Girard: Yes, as Kant said, human beings are charac-
terized by "asocial sociality." Here Kant is just developing the
insights of Thomas Hobbes and Jean-Jacques Rousseau—
those who romanticize social life are simply not grown up.

William James: Since I know more about the history of
psychology, let me attempt to situate your theory in terms of
other psychologists. According to Aristotle, whom you cite as
the pioneer of mimetic psychology, desires must be explained
in terms of their objects. For him, a potentiality is always
explained by an actuality; hence, the actual object of a desire is
what explains the potency of that desire. Every organism, says
Aristotle, is oriented toward what it perceives to be good—
even a plant grows toward the sun. We thus explain the
"desire" of a plant by the object it desires, in this case, the sun.
Or we explain the desire of an animal for food in terms of the
nutritive goodness of that object. According to Aristotle, a
desire, then, is a potential object; when the potential object is
actualized, the desire terminates. Furthermore, since every
organism is oriented toward what it perceives to be good,
every desire rests upon a belief, namely, that an object is good
for us. Desire is individuated by its objects.

René Girard: Yes, I reject Aristotle's fixed teleology of
desires because I see desire as a more basic energy that is essentially fungible: now fixed upon a woman, the same energy is
soon transferred to destroying my rival. Human desire is
open-ended and transferrable—like money. As for the idea
that desire somehow rests upon beliefs, I see beliefs as merely
rationalizations of prior desires; what we believe rests upon

our desires. I guess in this way I am more like Freud than like Aristotle.

William James: Like Freud, you see desire as formless energy that is fully fungible and transferrable. Freud's libido transfers from mouth to anus to genitals; it also shifts from mother to wife. But unlike both Freud and Aristotle, you don't see desire as intrinsic to an individual organism. For Freud and Aristotle, desire originates within the individual psyche and is directed to an object, imaginary or real. However, for you desire is the by-product of a triadic relationship between two human agents and one object. Desire emerges from triangular social situations, not from individual psyches.

René Girard: Yes, Romantic individualism tells us that our desires originate within our own souls, that each person is the author of his or her desires and that our desires reflect who we are. I reject all these claims in the strongest possible terms. Every human being is essentially like every other—an unpopular claim because it insults our pride. We desperately want to believe in our own uniqueness, but when asked what makes us unique, we all give the same answer. So we are all unique in the same way. Our deep faith in our own uniqueness explains the horror we feel in the presence of any kind of double, whether doppelganger, twin, clone, pod person, or bionic replica. From Greek myths to Dostoevsky to modern sci-fi, the monstrous double is the stuff of nightmare. Our desires differ not because human beings are essentially different but because our social situations differ. Anyone in a triangle becomes a rival, and anyone in a crowd looks for a scapegoat.

William James: Yes, here the contrast with Freud is particularly sharp since Freud posited primal instincts in each person toward pleasure, toward aggression, and toward death. What individuates us, he says, is a matter of how we express or sublimate these desires.

For Aristotle, desire and the good are equated: the good (real or merely apparent) is what all things desire. For you, on the other hand, desire and rivalry are equated: all rivalry is desirous and all desire is rivalrous.

René Girard: Explaining violence in terms of instinctive "aggression" is like explaining the effects of opium in terms of its dormitive powers. What could be more intellectually lazy than to explain conflict in terms of violent or aggressive impulses? How then is peace ever possible? Because we also have pacific instincts? What absurdity! There are no human instincts. We are by nature social animals, so we must look to the logic of social situations to account for our violence. What causes violence is not our inherent disposition toward violence but situations of rivalrous desire.

William James: Kurt Lewin, the great German social psychologist, argued that psychology must imitate the evolution of physics. Aristotelian physics was focused on the intrinsic properties of objects rather than on the relationships among objects. Aristotle explains the motion of bodies in terms of their inherent properties (heavy or light) rather than in terms of the field of forces acting upon them. In modern physics, on the contrary, not only is the "upward tendency" of a lighter body derived from the relation of this body to its environment, but the "weight" itself of the body depends upon such a relation. According to Lewin (who drew here upon his teacher, the great philosopher of science Ernst Cassirer), physics evolved from a focus on the nature of substances to a focus on the nature of fields. Lewin argued that the psychology of his day remained fundamentally Aristotelian because it attempted to explain behavior in terms of the predispositions, instincts, and drives of agents rather than in terms of the total field of forces operating in particular situations. Just as Aristotle explained the fall of a stone by its "heaviness," so he explained the behavior of individuals in terms of their natural instincts and acquired habits.

René Girard: Yes, I follow Lewin: conflict cannot be explained by features of individual persons. Conflict must be explained in terms of the triangular field of forces that arise between two agents and a common object. We must move from a naïvely dispositional psychology of personality to a truly social psychology of situations.

William James: But Lewin's actual social psychology is more complex than your simple situationism. Lewin was aware that a physical body partially creates the field of forces around it; he stressed the importance of the situation as jointly constituted by the object and its field, the person and the environment, and the figure and its ground. Just as he rejected explanations based on the isolated person, so would he reject explanations based on the situation alone. Lewin called for a social psychology that took into account both the dispositions of individuals and the situational field, since situations are partly shaped by dispositions and dispositions are partly shaped by situations. A social psychological field is therefore the joint product of individual dispositions and social relations.

So your conception of psychology is ultimately more purely social than Lewin's. For him, human agents are not merely interchangeable in the dynamics of social situations. Lewin would say that you need a theory of individual disposition and not just a theory of triangular social vectors if you want to explain conflict and violence.

René Girard: I do not deny the fact that individuals have various temperaments, dispositions, and habits. I just deny that the differences between people are significant enough to explain differences of conduct. Our urge to conform, to follow the crowd, to fit in—these social instincts overwhelm whatever qualities that individuate us. As Stanley Milgram and many other psychologists have shown, virtually anyone will violate his or her own moral code when placed in the wrong situation. How humbling to our pride to have to admit that we are not better than other people—just luckier. No wonder there is so much resistance to my "intervidual" psychology.

William James: Philosophers have also questioned the logic of your theory of desire. Paisley Livingston, for example, quotes you as saying that desire wills, intends, deceives itself, forgets, and so on. By ascribing these intentional acts to desire itself, Livingston argues, you have turned desire into a miniature person, a homunculus within each individual. Yet most philosophers consider desire to be but one faculty among several. Livingston even denies that you have a developed theory at all; he describes your work as a set of loosely connected and provocative hypotheses about psychology, sociology, and religion.

René Girard: I never claimed to be a philosopher and, in my view, there is often an inverse relationship between depth of insight and rigor of argumentation. It is foolish to expect logical rigor from the most profound thinkers or deep insights from the logic-choppers. There is no "Girardian system." I am simply teasing out the implications of one dense insight. Perhaps my training in literature has led me to use figurative rather than strictly literal language. I think this has often been frustrating for philosophers, who are tediously pedestrian when it comes to language.

William James: Speaking of metaphors, you often use infectious-disease metaphors to describe how we "catch" our desires: you often say, for example, that desire is "contagious." By this, you mean that desire is social in origin. However, contagions are not social phenomena but merely mass phenomena. Livingston argues that mimesis of any kind is the wrong starting point for understanding social life since, as Max Weber and others argue, social life involves persons who are subjectively oriented toward each other. Not only am I aware of you and are you aware of me, but I am aware that you are aware of me, and so forth. In this strategic situation, I act anticipating how you will react. But in mimesis, the model may not even be aware of the existence of the imitator, meaning that there is no social relation between them. Ironically, by denigrating human subjectivity as a mere Romantic myth, you undermine your ability to model actual social relations. You strive to build up an understanding of social life based purely on the objective convergence of desire and conduct—a convergence you attribute to mimesis, when in fact it can have many other sources as well. For example, you describe Don Quixote as imitating the desire of the legendary knight Amadis; and you say that Christians imitate the desire of Christ. Yet, perhaps Quixote's desire for chivalric honor is what led him to Amadis, just as the love of God can lead someone to Christ. In short, you claim that desire comes from imitating a model, but perhaps desire is what leads us to imitate a model.

Allow me to return to your French triangle. You say that a man desires a particular woman only because he sees another man desire her. But, as we know from social media, many men are often attracted to the same woman without any awareness of their rivals. Could not independent desires converge upon the same object? And the relation between rivals of the same woman is not based on imitation but on strategic intersubjectivity. Perhaps I flaunt my desire for her as a way to warn you to stay away? Perhaps I pretend not to desire her in order to see how much you desire her? Don't I act, in other words, always in awareness of what you are likely to think and to do? How does the simple notion of mimesis begin to capture the reality of strategic behavior and anticipated reactions?

René Girard: If social life were truly so strategic, intersubjective, and rational, we would not see so much irrational, contagious, and devastating mimetic conflict. When people are caught up in destructive rivalries they cannot even recall the original cause of the conflict; they are simply swept away by the contagion of violence. Each party to a rivalry behaves identically: each claims to be the victim of aggression by the other party. Everyone says: "He started it!" But the first thing we learn from the study of any rivalry is that all parties are fully interchangeable: there is no aggressor and no victim. Here Hobbes was right: moral language about who is right or wrong in these contexts is simply another weapon making the conflict even more deadly. Both parties are victims of the mimetic rivalry itself. I agree that some rivalries begin from strategic calculation, but all rational strategy is vaporized by the intensity of the escalating conflict. Soon, we lose sight of the original object and become obsessed with the destruction of our rival.

When we move from dyadic conflicts to scapegoating violence, the role of strategic intersubjectivity becomes even more negligible. When a crowd in the grip of witch-hunting, heretic-hunting, or anticommunist hysteria unanimously sets upon a random victim, we see no strategic rationality, just a diabolical convergence of desire and violence. In this case, however, the parties are not all interchangeable. The victim of the scapegoating violence alone sees the truth of the situation: that he is the victim of the crowd's desire for unanimity. Here there really is an aggressive crowd and an innocent victim. No one who participates in scapegoating violence could possibly see the victim as a scapegoat: that kind of subjective awareness is incompatible with the whole logic of scapegoating. We cannot create the unanimity and harmony of the lynch mob unless we are convinced that we are defending order and justice from a dangerous criminal or monster. Sometimes, participants in scapegoating violence come to realize that they were guilty of scapegoating, but only after the event. Such awareness is impossible during the scapegoating violence.

William James: We are getting ahead of ourselves here. Let's return to the notion of mimesis. You chose this Greek term in order to distinguish it from other related notions, but I am wondering how your mimesis compares with the ways that psychologists talk about imitation and other related behaviors.

René Girard: Mimesis is simply the basis of all human learning and, hence, of all human culture. Human beings are not born with a repertoire of adaptive instincts. In the absence of innate instincts, we can survive only by learning. As I like to remind our age of individualists, we are social animals who learn only by imitating others. So mimesis is simply another word for human learning and human enculturation. We learn from each other how to become human.

William James: Don't other animals also learn by imitation?

René Girard: Certainly. Primates clearly "ape" each other. But Aristotle was right when he said that man is the most mimetic of all animals since man has the greatest capacity for social learning.

William James: Actually, psychologists and ethologists question your view that all learning stems from imitation. One of my contemporaries, Edward L. Thorndike of Columbia University, pioneered the study of learning among primates. He found that imitation played a minor role in learning compared with the learning resulting from trial and error. In other words, researchers have established that among animals most learning is not social learning. Indeed, the very notion that all learning stems from imitation leads to a logical regress, for some animal must learn independently for innovation to be possible. So, yes, Aristotle is right that man is the most imitative of animals. But you are wrong that all learning, even among humans, stems from imitation.

René Girard: Well, perhaps I overstated the importance of imitation since psychologists and social scientists have deliberately ignored the centrality of mimesis during most of the twentieth century. Gabriel Tarde's great treatise, *The Laws of Imitation*, dates back to 1890. Why the long neglect of this central topic? I believe it is because acknowledging the role of imitation threatens our conception of ourselves as creative individuals. We like to believe that we are the source of our own desires and goals, that we are authors of our own lives.

William James: You could learn from Monsieur Tarde, who attributes all human social life to two fundamental principles: invention and imitation—thereby avoiding the logical regress generated by mimesis alone. If all desire were mimetic, then how could there be a new desire? You are right that the whole topic of imitation was strangely neglected for many decades, but since the 1970s there has been an explosion of new research. Once we see how psychologists and ethologists understand imitation, I think we shall see how implausible is the idea of mimetic desire. As it turns out, desire is the one thing that cannot be imitated. Ethologists and anthropologists, when observing animal and human behavior, have distinguished three distinct kinds of mimesis. True imitation is defined as learning a task by observing and then copying both the means and the goal of the model. This kind of mimesis is cognitively demanding. No animal has been observed to truly imitate another animal except for primates who are trained by humans to do so. Another form of mimesis, emulation, is defined as learning to accomplish a goal by observing another animal without copying the means to that goal. Many animals have been observed learning by emulation. Lastly, mimicry is the capacity of one animal to replicate the means of another animal without accomplishing the same goal. A parrot can mimic human speech but not emulate or imitate human speech since a parrot has no communicative intentions. Children take delight in mimicking adults, and adults love the voice impressions of a mimic. Imitation, emulation, and mimicry logically exhaust all true forms of mimesis. Mimicry is the first, most fundamental, and most universal form of mimesis. Emulation is widespread among mammals and especially among primates. Imitation is restricted to human beings and to animals trained by human beings.

René Girard: I discuss literary and living examples of all these kinds of mimesis. But I am most interested in the phenomenon of contagious desire or what I call "mimetic snowballing." In these cases, we unconsciously and instantaneously copy the desires of those around us. This is how tit-for-tat violence as well as the flocking behavior of murderous crowds emerges.

William James: Yes, social contagion and flocking behavior are found among human beings. But they do not involve any kind of imitation, emulation, or even mimicry. Laughter, anger, yawning, and smiling are known to be contagious among people—not because anyone is copying anyone else but because seeing or hearing these affects triggers our own affective responses. When we flock together by laughing or yawning, your behavior triggers my own, but I am not copying any particular person. Such "response priming" does not involve any kind of imitation because nothing new is learned. Contagious behavior does not teach us anything; it just causes us to join the flock. In this contagion, we are not engaged in selecting models whose desires we imitate; rather, we are caught up in a net of triggered responses. Just as yawns and laughter spread through a crowd, so do panic and violence. Imitation, emulation, and mimicry are all focused on particular models, which provide tokens of a general type of behavior. Contagious and flocking behavior, by contrast, involve the spread of general types of behavior without the imitation of any particular token. What this means is that generalized types of behavior can spread among people without any kind of mimesis. In short, there is no such thing as "mimetic snowballing." Mimetic behavior is not contagious, and contagious behavior is not mimetic.

René Girard: Your argument that social contagion does not involve mimesis rests upon a rather subtle distinction between general model-types and specific model-tokens. I think most of us will regard that as a piece of sophistry. Moreover, your distinction between mimesis and social contagion rests upon a fallacious assumption that mimesis is intentional—in contrast to clearly unintentional flocking behavior. But I have learned from Tarde that our intentional conduct is only the visible part of a much larger and submerged iceberg of unconscious behavior. All mimesis, I argue, is to some degree contagious and unconscious. For example, we know from the study of mirror neurons that the neurons activated when we observe certain actions are also activated when we perform them. What this means is that every human being is neurologically primed to imitate the types of behavior we see around us. This applies to all forms of what you call mimesis, not merely social contagions. Yet we allow even children to watch movies full of violence, ignoring the undeniable way in which observing violence primes us for violence. All desire is not only mimetic but also rivalrous. Rivalry and desire are coextensive. For this reason, social contagion always ultimately leads to violent conflagration.

William James: A few more examples will show, I think, that social contagion has no necessary relation to any form of imitation, not even mimicry. I am not denying that many kinds of social contagion also involve motor mimicry; I merely deny that social contagions necessarily involve motor mimicry. First, Adam Smith gives the example of witnessing a blow directed to another man's arm: we instinctively withdraw our own arm even if the victim does not. Similarly, if we see someone lean over a precipice, we lean back. Second, Darwin gives the example of listening to a lecture by someone with a cold. We instinctively cough even if the speaker is merely congested. We cough on his or her behalf. Third, I submit the well-known cases of "folie à deux" in which the psychotic symptoms (usually delusions) of one person are transferred to another person. These forms of behavior are clearly contagious but they involve no imitation: there are no models and no copies. Instead, a deep form of emotional sympathy causes our sentiments and conduct to converge. These patterns of convergence are sometimes called flocking behavior. Birds converge in flight formations without mimicking each other; similarly, our social conversations, our postures, vocal tones, facial expressions, and general demeanor tend to converge.

You see these patterns of imitation and social contagion as leading inexorably to rivalry, conflict, and violence. But psychologists see social contagion and flocking behavior as leading not to conflict but to greater affiliation. Social contagion both reflects and causes pro-social and cooperative behavior. In general, we feel friendly toward those with whom we flock together. I see no basis for your dire rhetoric regarding the inevitability of violent conflagration.

René Girard: If conversation is supposed to lead to emotional convergence and affiliation, then why is our conversation becoming an intellectual fight to the death? I'd say that our behavior fits my theory better than it fits yours.

William James: Are you suggesting that Socratic discussion aimed at finding the truth often leads to a fight to dominate one's discussion partner? Is philosophy the moral equivalent of war?

With some trepidation, I propose that we peacefully examine the idea that one could imitate the desire of another person. Recall that imitation, emulation, and mimicry all involve observing or listening to a model-token. But how can one possibly observe or hear the desire of one's model? Desire is not observable and hence not a possible object of mimesis.

René Girard: What a canard! Nothing is more common, in life or in law, than inferring the desire of another person from observing his or her behavior. If I observe someone repeatedly shooting another person point-blank, I can safely infer a desire to kill that person. If I observe someone chopping wood, I can infer that he desires to heat his home. If I observe someone making love to a woman, I can infer that he desires her. So, if we can infer desires from observed behavior, then surely we can imitate desires. Advertisers ply us with models whom we see enjoying various commodities; we are meant to imitate not merely their actions but also their desires. By the way, Tarde also insisted that the primary target of imitation is the desire of the model.

William James: Yes and no. In life and in law we often distinguish between intentions and motives. We noted that imitation means copying both the goals and the means of the model; you are right that the goal of an action can often be inferred from the means. When one animal sees another hitting a coconut with a rock, it infers that the goal is to open it and eat the meat inside. If desire means merely the intention of an action, then, yes, imitation and emulation do involve mimetic desire. But things get more complicated with human conduct, in which the same intention is compatible with many different motives. Let's begin with your lovely example of deliberate killing. Yes, seeing such violence does allow us to infer that the shooter intended to kill his victim; clearly, this was no accident or case of mere negligence. But why did the killer intend to kill? Was his motive revenge? Jealousy? Racism? Self-defense? Or political ideology? If we think of desire in terms of these deeper motives—and I think we must—then we cannot reliably infer motives from mere observation. Take the man chopping wood. Surely he intends to produce logs, but what is his motive? To get exercise? To impress his girlfriend? To punish himself? To earn money? Or to heat his home? Human desire includes both motive and intention: when I imitate someone's bare intention I can hardly be said to imitate that person's underlying desire. Desire as motivation is simply not available to the would-be imitator. As Livingston points out, your own example of advertisements undermines your whole notion of mimetic desire since it is obvious that the models we see in ads do not actually desire the relevant commodities: they only pretend to desire them.

René Girard: I think human beings have the capacity to infer actual motives quite reliably. Our capacity to grasp the thoughts and motives of other persons goes far beyond the simplistic rational deductions you describe. We don't work so inductively from gesture to intention to motive; instead, we grasp the tenor of another person's desires holistically. Even a dog knows the difference between being kicked and being stumbled over. As Monsieur Tarde famously observes, imitation works from the inside out (*ab interioribus ad exteriora*): we intuit the deep desire and use it to predict the observable gesture. I know this sounds suspiciously like telepathy, but I think it true of our amazing abilities to read minds. The social contagion of anorexia shows that young women understand perfectly well the motive behind the act of not eating; they do not confuse the desire to lose weight with the desire to fast.

William James: In the case of anorexia, the real puzzle is why these women want to lose so much weight. Are they motivated by an envy of supermodels? Self-loathing? Or the desire to gain control over their bodies? I agree that the intention to lose weight can be imitated, but what about the deeper motivations? Is not the desire to lose weight unintelligible apart from those deeper motives? If so, how is it possible to truly imitate desire?

Livingston argues on other grounds that no desire can be fully imitated since every agent has a different relationship to the object of imitation. Let's take your own example of the Tenth Commandment: "You shall not covet your neighbor's wife nor anything else that belongs to your neighbor." According to you, this prohibition is meant to suppress mimetic desire: we desire our neighbor's wife and possessions because he desires them. But even if we correctly infer the reasons why our neighbor desires what he possesses, we cannot imitate his desire because what he desires is his own lawful wife and possessions, whereas what we desire is another man's wife and possessions. Because two agents can never have the same relationship to any object of desire—one of them by definition got there first—one person cannot copy another person's desire.

René Girard: By mimesis I certainly do not mean exact replication of a desire-token, to use your own language. Instead, I mean only the triggering of a desire of the same generic type as in the model. As I have said, the science of mirror neurons reveals that when I observe your actions, the same neurons are activated in my brain as when I perform an action of the same type. In other words, observing an action and performing that action are neurologically equivalent. And, since actions get their species from their intentions, when I imitate your actions, I am imitating your intentions as well as your physical motions. In short, the science of mirror neurons has revealed the physiological basis for my notion of mimetic desire.

William James: I want to examine a special case of mimetic desire, one that has occupied a great deal of your attention lately. This is the case of tit-for-tat reciprocity.

René Girard: Yes, I explored this kind of behavior in my book on Clausewitz. Nothing focuses the mind like the prospect of a hanging. Well, the nuclear arms race represented for my generation the prospect of the total annihilation of the human race. Clausewitz helps us to understand how rational strategy quickly degenerates into mutually-assured destruction. He famously defined war as "the continuation of politics by other means." But this definition applies only to the decision to wage war. Once the war has begun, a whole new dynamic takes over, one that has no relation to the pursuit of any political goal. The conflict "escalates to extremes." Whatever political goal we once pursued is soon eclipsed by the overwhelming desire to destroy the rival—even at the cost of self-destruction. Military victories tend to be Pyrrhic. What interests me about this logic of escalation is that both parties are locked into a dynamic that leads them ineluctably to where they don't want to go. Violence has its own logic quite independent of the rational aims of the individuals involved. Military planners such as Herman Kahn live in a dream world of strategic rationality. In Kahn's model of nuclear confrontation, there are sixty stages of escalation! Yet we all know that these conflicts will escalate not by careful rational calibration but by a rapid descent into total Armageddon.

William James: I must object to your one-sided reading of Clausewitz, whose theory of war is a complex dialectic between theoretical tendencies and practical realities. Yes, war has a logical tendency to escalate to extremes, but in practice this tendency is often counterbalanced by the realities of "friction"—namely, weather, ignorance, incompetence, and fear. Moreover, Clausewitz believes that leadership of genius can prevent war from overstepping its rational political objectives.

Nonetheless, I agree that you have identified a genuinely puzzling and, much worse, destructively irrational phenomenon. Clausewitz aside, I want to understand how you explain this "escalation to extremes."

René Girard: All reciprocity rests upon mimetic desire. I reach my hand out to you and you copy me by reaching out your own hand; I withdraw my hand, and then you withdraw yours. I snub you, then you snub me. Reciprocity makes no sense apart from mimetic desire: why should I respond to a gesture with the same type of gesture? Let's take the example of the gift. As Marcel Mauss shows in his classic essay, all gifts are exchanges: I give so that you will give *(do ut des)*. My desire to give triggers your desire to give, so we exchange gifts. Sometimes it is considered rude to give back immediately, so I wait to reciprocate. But apart from mimetic desire, I see no way to explain the universal reciprocity of gift giving. It is easy to explain economic reciprocity in terms of self-interest, but how does one explain the reciprocity of gifts?

Some kinds of reciprocity, of course, are not so benign. In duels, we see violent reciprocity and often fatal escalation. Each party mirrors the other: proper blows are met by proper blows, improper by improper. But as desire for the contentious object recedes and desire for eliminating the rival grows, the conflict escalates. In war, atrocity is mirrored by counter-atrocity. Hitler broke all the laws of war by terror-bombing civilians, so the Allies, to their everlasting shame, mirrored Hitler by terror-bombing German civilians. By the way, it is clear that the Allies copied not just Nazi tactics but also Nazi desire: the Allies formed an explicit policy of killing as many German civilians as technically possible. There is a profound proverb that captures this strange kind of mimesis: "choose your enemies carefully because you will become like them." How else to explain the universal descent into barbarism we saw during the war?

William James: Yes, during the course of a duel or war, the opponents do converge in their behavior. We become, willy-nilly, what we most hate. I don't know how to explain this. It challenges the simple idea that violence is a tool that we wield for our own purposes. It seems more accurate to say that we are tools deployed by violence for purposes not our own.

Here are my doubts that mimetic desire can explain reciprocity. The theory of mimetic desire would lead us to expect symmetrical reciprocity. However, reciprocity is never

perfectly symmetrical: we call it "tit for tat" not "tat for tat."
Even in routine greetings, it would appear robotic to replay the
same gesture offered to us. When the first person breaks the
ice, it is customary to respond with a gesture slightly more
friendly. Gifts are not usually identical: the wealthier party is
expected to give more, and to reciprocate with an identical gift,
as in "re-gifting," violates the norms of the gift. When it comes
to violent reciprocity, then we see escalation, which by definition is not mimetic. With pure mimesis we would not expect
escalation, which always involves innovation by one party. I
don't see how this innovation can be explained by mimetic
desire.

Reciprocity can be explained only with concepts that
involve intersubjective awareness: I do not imitate you from
the outside, but I empathize with you from the inside. I give
while knowing what it feels like to be a receiver. Social scientists call this the "law of anticipated reaction," and it forms the
basis of reciprocity. First, due to a universal sense of justice,
when we do things for other people, we expect them to do
things for us. Second, we use reciprocity to get another person
to do what we want. I give a gift knowing that the receiver will
feel a general obligation to me in the future. If I expected
exactly the same gift in return, then I would not have given a
gift but would have just made a swap. A good gift does not
copy the original gift but merely expresses the same goodwill
in a new way.

You describe escalation as returning a gift "with interest."
But where does this "interest" come from? Again, if conflicts
were truly mimetic, then there would be no escalation: we
would just have the eternal return of the same. Escalation
means innovation, not imitation. Conflict is based on strategic
reciprocity in which each person acts based on his anticipation
of the reaction of his opponents. If my opponent kills fifty of
my men, then I might kill fifty of his men—not because I am
locked into an automatic mimesis but because I anticipate that
an equal reprisal will stop his killing. If I thought that killing
more than fifty would stop him, then I would kill more than
fifty, but I fear that a disproportionate reprisal might just escalate, rather than stop, the killing. As a rational strategy,

reciprocity depends upon my knowing what my opponent wants and knowing that my opponent knows that I know what he wants, and so on. I don't see what any of this inter-subjectivity has to do with mimesis.

René Girard: Naturally, I do not deny the importance of intersubjective awareness to complex forms of reciprocity. My claim is that intersubjectivity rests upon a pre-reflective foundation of mimesis. Were we not predisposed to imitate the gestures, facial expressions, and moods of our companions we would not be able to engage in more complex forms of reciprocity. We unconsciously return the eye contact and the smile before we choose a greeting. We see the priority of mimetic reciprocity in evolution and in human development: animal mimicry and flocking long predates the emergence of inter-subjective reciprocity; infants learn to mimic the expressions of their mothers long before they learn how to converse. Everywhere, intersubjective awareness rests upon a mimetic foundation. We would not trust our companions in the first place had mimesis not done its work to cause our gestures and desires to converge. As for "mimetic escalation to extremes," what is being imitated is not the particular gesture but the desire to destroy. Escalation does not involve a simple mimicry of the previous offer but the imitation of my opponent's desire to destroy me.

William James: I want to explore the notion of a model in your theory. Cervantes chose Amadis as the model for his desires while a Christian imitates Christ. We desire according to the other, and the other is a model for our desire. Livingston shows that, far from being logically primitive, mimetic desire itself rests upon what he calls "tutelary" desires and beliefs: before I can copy someone else's desires, I must desire to be like my model. We do not choose our role models randomly. You argue that a knight imitates a chivalric model, while a Christian imitates Christ, but you never attempt to explain why one person desires to be a knight while another desires to be a Christian. So, at a minimum, we can see that not all desire is mimetic because mimesis itself rests upon prior tutelary desires. Our desire to become like our role model is not a desire we can copy from someone else because before we copy anyone we must desire to become like them. So how do we account for these prior tutelary desires and beliefs that lead us to want to imitate a model? These questions take on urgent existential import in your latest apocalyptic statements that the crisis of modern violence forces humanity to choose between self-destruction and the imitation of Christ. But before we can imitate Christ we must desire to imitate him. Where does that desire come from?

René Girard: I have not always distinguished clearly enough between conscious and unconscious mimesis. Yes, in terms of conscious, deliberate mimesis, Livingston is right that I must first form a desire (which includes relevant beliefs) to be like a model. I do not discuss these tutelary desires and beliefs; I am grateful to Livingston for supplementing my work in this respect. But a good deal of mimesis, I argue, does not rest upon the deliberate selection of a model. This is the phenomenon of what you call "response priming" or flocking behavior—and what I call "contagious" desire or "mimetic snowballing." Zoologists and social psychologists have well established that mere physical proximity to other members of the same species leads organisms to converge their behavior and mood in a variety of ways. I now see this unconscious mimesis as mainly responsible for generating the crisis of violence and the search for a scapegoat.

William James: Yes, I can see how these sub-rational, contagious desires do not rest upon tutelary desires. But your theory is now less coherent because you are using the concept of mimesis to describe two fundamentally different kinds of desire-formation: on the one hand, we have the literary models of the French triangle and on the other, the biology of social contagion. Your argument as a whole appears to fail from equivocation. Also, if unconscious mimetic snowballing is chiefly responsible for the crisis of violence, then how is the conscious choice to imitate Christ a solution? In some places, you even deny the possibility of making a rational choice between role models: "In fact there is no way of distinguishing on an objective basis . . . between forms of behavior that are 'good' to imitate and those that are not." If we are thus locked into mimetic behavior without any ability to choose our models wisely, then we can never escape the fatal logic of mimetic conflict. Without a theory of tutelary desires, conscious mimetic desire is left without a foundation, and the modern crisis of violence is left without a solution.

René Girard: To preserve the coherence of my thought, I guess I must bite this bullet and deny a fundamental distinction between conscious and unconscious desire-formation. Whether they are Don Quixote, Emma Bovary, or *Jules et Jim*, people have desires that are formed by unconscious contagion. They do not deliberately choose their role models, so they need no tutelary desires or beliefs. The whole notion of better or worse role models does not arise if desire is randomly contagious. Even the desire to imitate Christ is not chosen but is merely an unmerited gift of grace. So, yes, on this understanding of contagious desire, there is no rational solution to the crisis of violence—only hope for divine salvation.

William James: That outcome is profoundly disappointing to those of us who looked to your work for a remedy and not merely a diagnosis of the crisis of violence.

But even more disappointing is your total neglect of the work of my brother, Henry. His novels are chock-full of French triangles, social rivalry, envy, and all manner of competitive desire. Do you have something against Henry? As a European who lived long in America, I thought you would be attracted to an American who lived long in Europe.

René Girard: Yes, I know Henry's novels well, and I admire them. Indeed, given my view of the cognitive value of great literature, I am bound to say that Henry is the true psychologist in your family.

CHAPTER FOUR

A Crowd of Theories

René Girard: What a delight to talk about crowds and scapegoats with the great social psychologist, Gordon Allport, who has written about the psychology of scapegoating, and with Elias Canetti, a Nobel Laureate in Literature and author of the magisterial *Crowds and Power*. My friend Sigmund Freud, who needs no introduction, has agreed to join us as well. Feel free to gang up against me; I am accustomed to it! By the end of our conversation, I am sure you will all be fast friends. From the conference room of our Paris hotel, we enjoy a spectacular view of Place de la Concorde. What a splendid name for a public square infamous for so many scapegoat murders during the Revolution—for, yes, killing the scapegoat does indeed lay the foundation for peace. I think I can see Madame Defarge . . .

Gordon Allport: I want to thank René for bringing the terrible scandal of scapegoating to our attention. Indeed, he is responsible for popularizing the term *lynchage* in contemporary French. No one can deny the reality of scapegoating. Every human being has felt a desire to vent his or her frustration upon totally innocent victims. Indeed, sometimes we even "punish" inanimate objects. Yet we often hide this ugly and irrational impulse under layers of rationalization to the effect that the chosen victim somehow deserves our unwarranted abuse. Dad is more likely to kick the family dog after a stressful day at work; similarly, social groups and even whole nations are more likely to choose arbitrary scapegoats when they are under severe pressure, especially in time of war, famine, or plague. This impulse to find and to victimize scapegoats has caused unfathomable suffering for racial and religious minorities since the dawn of history.

René Girard: Gordon, I reject your attempt to reduce the social phenomenon of scapegoating to the individual psychology of frustration and aggression. Kicking the family dog has nothing to do with the social reality of scapegoating, which has the function of creating social unity, not venting frustration. Only social groups are capable of scapegoating, though the victims of scapegoating can be either individual persons or minority groups. Sometimes Captain Dreyfus is the victim and sometimes it is the whole Jewish race. But the scapegoater must always be a social group since the whole point of scapegoating is to create social harmony. Nothing—absolutely nothing—brings people together like killing an innocent victim. Even groups absolutely riven with violent conflict within their ranks will experience profound harmony when they find and kill a scapegoat. The Gospel reports that after scapegoating Jesus, Pilate and Herod—who had been enemies—suddenly became friends. All other forms of social harmony are trivial or illusory compared to the harmony created by the death of the scapegoat. Scapegoating is a social not a psychological fact.

Gordon Allport: Just because psychology and sociology are sharply divided within the academy does not mean they are separable in real life. What basis could the sociology of scapegoating have if it is not rooted in individual psychology? How could we explain the propensity of the French nation to scapegoat Dreyfus or the propensity of white Americans to scapegoat Japanese-Americans without reference to individual motives? These motives can include frustration, guilt evasion, fear, anxiety, self-enhancement, desire for conformity, and so on. Individuals have many possible motives for participating in scapegoating, but I see no other way to explain social scapegoating except by reference to these individual motives. We know from many other phenomena in social and political psychology that individuals can agree upon a common goal for very different reasons. Hence, individuals with widely different kinds of motives can come together in the common project of a lynching.

What all scapegoaters must share is the belief that the victim is guilty. Scapegoating would not be satisfying if we feared that the scapegoat could be innocent. I am convinced that scapegoaters are absolutely, though often catastrophically, sincere in their belief that their victim is guilty and, hence, deserves punishment. Indeed, scapegoating is only rousing and satisfying if it stems from righteous indignation. We love the feeling of moral superiority as we play the role of judge, jury, and executioner. In short, scapegoating is an example of the joys of moralistic aggression, which range from backbiting to rebuke to revenge. Human nature is basically good, which is why we enjoy evil only when it is dressed up as justice.

René Girard: I do not share your rosy view of human nature. Many people are attracted to scapegoating—even if they know the victim is innocent—because scapegoating is the one opportunity most people have to kill with full impunity. Normally, we are restrained from killing by the fear of retaliation or punishment. But who would miss an opportunity to kill with impunity? Nonetheless, I agree with you that scapegoating cannot fulfill its social function of creating harmony unless the crowd believes the victim is guilty. I call this necessary delusion *méconnaissance*. Because guilt is a metaphysical reality not directly observable, crowds look for signs of guilt, the stigmata of the victim, which can include deformity, disease, being a twin, or even "diabolical" cleverness (as with Oedipus). Since the community unites around its persecution of the victim, the victim is usually someone who can be seen as outside or at least marginal to the community.

Gordon Allport: True, the victim must be accessible and weak: a scapegoat is a safegoat. But surely the key question is how to stop scapegoating, since we seem to agree that scapegoating is irrational. I think we should consider these possible remedies for this scourge: education about the dangers of scapegoating (with vivid historical examples), public policy measures to ensure greater economic security, and laws to prevent any discrimination against vulnerable and unpopular minorities.

René Girard: Your proposed remedies for scapegoating are ludicrously naïve about the reality of social order. We cannot possibly remove scapegoating from the existing social order without causing much worse forms of violence to erupt. Scapegoating, after all, functions to redirect violent impulses that would otherwise destroy society entirely. Let us recall what leads to scapegoating: mimetic desire. Because desire is mimetic, desire is also inevitably rivalrous. The anarchy of deadly competition over rival goods threatens a "war of all against all." Not only is violence contagious but, through cycles of revenge, violence tends to escalate. Such a conflagration of one-on-one conflicts can be avoided only if the community unites against a single victim. If one person or a small minority can be credibly accused of causing the conflicts threatening social harmony, then a community riven with myriad internal conflicts can suddenly unite against a perceived outsider. Scapegoat violence, then, is normally medicinal: it protects and immunizes a community from the much more destructive and anarchic crisis of violence. Scapegoat violence is good violence needed to protect us from the bad violence of Hobbesian anarchy. One can fight fire only with fire, bad violence only with good violence. Scapegoat murder is an economical use of violence to sublimate and control chaotic and escalating violence. The high priest Caiaphas, for example, explained the necessity of Jesus's execution: "It is better for one man to die than for the whole nation to perish." Throughout history, societies have institutionalized scapegoat violence through the use of capital punishment. Whole communities unite around the killing of a victim, often with little real concern for his or her guilt or innocence. Without these violent rituals, we would be consumed in tit-for-tat escalating conflicts. Your proposed remedies are not remotely adequate to the danger that mimetic rivalry poses to social order. Have you ever seen how petty insults can escalate into duels, feuds, and atrocities? You may see scapegoating as a superfluous evil to be corrected; I see scapegoating as the foundation of society.

Gordon Allport: Your description of the scapegoat has shifted over time. In your book *Violence and the Sacred*, you describe the "surrogate-victim" as chosen randomly or arbitrarily. And in *The Scapegoat*, you argue that lynching creates social unity whether the victim is a guilty rapist or Marie Antoinette. If the function of scapegoating is to create social harmony around the persecution of a victim, all that matters is that the crowd perceives the scapegoat to be guilty. Whether the scapegoat is actually innocent or guilty is irrelevant to the function of scapegoating. Just as Durkheim said that there are no false religions, since they all serve the same function, so you must say that there are no false scapegoats, since every scapegoat serves its function. But, later, you argued that because Jesus was himself the victim of a scapegoat murder, the Bible reveals the truth that the scapegoat victim is always innocent. I don't see how this moralism about "innocent victims" is compatible with your functional theory of scapegoating. In the case of Robespierre or, more recently, of Saddam Hussein, we see that guilty men frequently become victims of scapegoating murder.

René Girard: I should have made clearer that over time I uncovered three points of view about the scapegoat: from the point of view of social function, the actual guilt or innocence of the scapegoat is irrelevant, so long as the crowd believes that he is guilty; from the point of view of myth, which takes the perspective of the persecutors, the scapegoat is guilty; from the point of view of the Gospels, which takes the perspective of the victims, the scapegoat is actually innocent. How to reconcile the Gospel truth about the innocence of the victim with the functional truth about an arbitrary victim? Clearly, the crowd believes that the victim is guilty, not merely of some particular crime, but of causing social conflict in general; the crowd believes that killing the victim will restore social unity. These beliefs clearly rest upon *méconnaissance*. The cause of social conflict is mimetic desire itself, not some particular person; killing a person or even a group of people may create a temporary feeling of harmony but no lasting peace. This is the truth of the Gospel: not that all scapegoats are without sin, merely that they are innocent of causing the crisis of violence. Let him who has no mimetic desire cast the first stone. The Gospel teaches us that killing never creates a durable peace.

By the way, the spread of Christianity has torn off the veil of *méconnaissance*. Because God himself was the victim of a scapegoat murder, it is increasingly difficult for modern men to believe that scapegoats are actually guilty, which is one reason why our contemporary world is suffering from a crisis of violence. The traditional remedies are no longer effective—

Elias Canetti (interrupting): Enough with the scapegoats! We live in such an appalling culture of aggrieved victimhood. The Irish, Poles, Jews, and now the blacks all compete over who is the most oppressed people ever (M.O.P.E.)—not an attractive form of rivalry. Being a scapegoat is now a point of pride; social stigmas are the new form of heraldry. Australians, who make up a nation of scapegoats, brag about their descent from convicts: "chosen by the best judges in England." Girard's theory creates the theoretical foundations for our contemporary festival of victimization, despite his recent attempts to distance himself from what he has wrought. Girard argues that the central message of the Bible is the truth of the victim. According to Girard, God himself became a victim of scapegoating on the cross, and we should imitate him!

Gordon Allport: The victim who survives is the hero of our age. In the past, when relatively few people were killed, a hero died for his cause, like Socrates or Jesus. But in our age of mass extermination, a hero is someone who survives for his cause, like Viktor Frankl or Aleksandr Solzhenitsyn. Where millions are killed, what is heroic is not dying but surviving. Hence, from Holocaust and Gulag survivor, we now have rape survivor, sexual abuse survivor, racism survivor, and microaggression survivor.

René Girard: Far from providing a foundation for our modern cult of victimhood, my theory alone can explain it. What could be more mimetic than the current rivalry of victim-hood? The "truth of the victim" is the insight that we must reject the whole logic of scapegoating; this truth emerged only when Jesus assumed the role of victim. In arguing for the truth of the victim against the lie of the accuser, I should have made it clearer that actual victims in history tend to pivot rather quickly into the role of accuser. Tragically, few victims ever understand the truth of the victim. Although St. Paul evolved from persecutor to victim, many early Christians evolved from victims to persecutors. And historians of the Holocaust argue that many victims of Stalin's persecution pivoted instantly to become agents of Nazi persecution. So actually being a victim may be necessary but is certainly not sufficient for grasping the truth of the victim. A bitter irony of our contemporary culture of aggrieved victimhood is that most victims are ready to accuse a scapegoat.

Elias Canetti: The scapegoat or "surrogate-victim" draws our attention and sympathy but distracts us from the heart of Girard's theory, which is a theory of crowds. Let us recall Girard's claims that all social order stems from the unity of a lynch mob and that this lynch mob is also the hidden foundation of all religious rituals today. These are striking—even startling—claims until we understand Girard's theory of crowds in its proper French context. Girard himself, not to mention his commentators, discusses his ideas by explicitly referencing many great thinkers: Plato, Aristotle, Hobbes, Rousseau, Nietzsche, Durkheim, and Freud. But Girard actually developed his ideas in relation to a line of obscure but important French theorists of imitation in social life: Gabriel Tarde, Gustave Le Bon, and Paul Guillaume. Like many modern social theorists, including Durkheim, Girard suppressed his indebtedness to these minor and, in the case of Le Bon, partly discredited figures. We can see Girard's deep indebtedness to these French theorists in his key concepts: from Tarde he acquired "imitative desire" (mimetic desire) and "interpsychology" (what Girard calls "intervidual psychology"); from Le Bon "crowd contagion;" and from Guillaume the idea that "the object seems desirable only because it is coveted by someone else," as well as the example of two children vying for the same toy. Here is Girard's true milieu, not the parade of philosophical giants usually trotted out. Tarde, Le Bon, and Durkheim all see the crowd as the template of social life and as the seedbed of religion. Girard's contribution to social thought can only be understood in relation to this French tradition.

René Girard (turning to Allport): Why do I get the sinking feeling that we are about to be treated to a display of Teutonic learning?

Elias Canetti: Don't panic. I'll stick to the basic theoretical logic of crowd analysis. Crowds have always been at the center of social and political theory. Unfortunately, in the theoretical literature crowds have often been conflated with social classes or with the masses, as in David Riesman's *Lonely Crowd*. But I will contrast an active crowd with a passive social class or mass of men; a social class or mass is only a potential crowd. As John McClelland shows, political philosophy begins with Plato's effort to show that democracy ultimately means rule by a violent mob. With his unparalleled poetic gifts, Plato gives classic expression to aristocratic disdain for and fear of crowds by comparing them to wild beasts—they are powerful, dangerous, impulsive, and irrational. Of course, Plato also thought that the poor working men who made up the crowd were driven by impulse and appetite, so his crowd is just an irrational person writ large, and an individual worker is just a beastly crowd writ small. Most crowd theorists, however, see the crowd as different in nature from its individual components—usually worse but sometimes better.

If a deliberative assembly can be regarded as a crowd (a closed crowd, in my terms), then Aristotle thought that the assembly was often better and wiser than its individual constituents due to the deliberative process. But the Romans had a counter-maxim that "senators are good men but the Senate, a wild beast." Here we see the puzzle: If crowds are made up exclusively of individual men, then how can they act in ways that are much worse (or sometimes much better) than the acts of the men who make them up? One recent version of this puzzle is what economists call "the wisdom of crowds," which is best illustrated by Francis Galton's observation of eight hundred Englishmen independently estimating the weight of an ox. The mean of those estimates was within one pound of the true weight, meaning that the "crowd" was more accurate than any expert. At first glance, this case appears similar to Aristotle's example of how the many can be wiser than the few. But in Aristotle's example, the many become wise from sharing in debate and deliberation, while in Galton's example the many are wise only when each person makes his or her guess without consulting anyone else. Only an economist could call a set of people who never communicate with each other a crowd.

Gordon Allport: Yes, the puzzle of how a crowd differs from its members is what gave birth to the disciplines of sociology and social psychology in nineteenth-century France.

Elias Canetti: Quite right. I'll take the hint and fast-forward my history to the French Revolution. Not since the Roman bread riots have crowds played a more salient role in the political imaginary than did the Parisian crowds of Place de la Concorde, le Bastille, and the like. Why are the French especially known for the political violence of their crowds? I believe that the average Frenchman does not trust even elected officials to truly "represent" his views, so he insists upon representing himself at the barricades. From 1789 to 1871, Paris and other French cities were bloody battlegrounds between Revolutionary and Counter-Revolutionary crowds.

It says a lot about the reputation of crowds that the modern social psychology of crowds was pioneered by the criminologists Scipio Sighele and Gabriel Tarde. They wondered how crowds of criminals could commit atrocities unthinkable to the persons who made them up. At the end of the nineteenth century, French bourgeois and aristocratic fear and loathing of crowds peaked just when Gustave Le Bon, an amateur social scientist lacking any academic position, generalized and popularized the nascent science of crowds in his phenomenal bestseller *The Crowd*. Le Bon seemed to capture precisely this tense and transitional moment in French (and broadly European) history when, as he says, "the divine right of the masses is about to replace the divine right of kings." His book was perhaps the most influential work of social science ever published. Theodore Roosevelt travelled to Paris to meet Le Bon; Hitler and Mussolini studied his work assiduously. Le Bon was the first to fully articulate the widespread fear of crowds and to offer a seemingly scientific explanation of why they are so dangerous. True, he borrowed most of his theories from the criminology of Sighele and Tarde, but he also applied them more broadly to all kinds of crowds. According to Le Bon, crowds have their own minds quite separate from the minds of the individuals who make them up. Crowds have their own distinctive psychology, their own distinctive passions and ideas. To characterize this crowd mind, Le Bon appealed to a panoply of mutually incompatible ideas: the crowd mind is the unconscious mind of the individual and the racial unconscious of mankind. Indeed, the crowd mind is a reversion to the mind of primitive man. The crowd mind, he says, is deeply stupid, credulous, impulsive, and fanatic; in a crowd, rational individuals become primitive savages and unruly children.

How does the crowd mind emerge? Here Le Bon borrows from Tarde and appeals to the prestige of the new science of hypnotism. He argues that individuals are hypnotized by the crowd or by the leader of the crowd. Human suggestibility and our innate drive to imitate induces conscious, rational men to become unconscious savages when mesmerized by the hypnotic power of the crowd and its leader. Many Europeans had seen the power of hypnosis in music-hall entertainment. Moreover, at the time hypnosis enjoyed wide scientific interest and prestige. So Le Bon's appeal to the hypnotic power of crowds to explain "collective hallucinations" gave his theory persuasive power among intellectuals as well as among the broader reading public. Consider the analogy: Once in a trance, the subject is blind and deaf to anyone but the hypnotist, just as members of a crowd are blind to anyone but their leader. Tarde had already asserted that most human beings are so conformist, so suggestible, they could be called sleep-walkers. Le Bon just made this idea more palatable by limiting somnambulism to crowds. It is easy to make fun of these passé nineteenth-century notions of mesmerism, hypnotism, and magnetism. But anyone who has witnessed Hitler's power over a crowd is likely to refer precisely to mesmerism, hypnotism, and magnetism.

René Girard: Yes, *comme tout le monde*, I have read Le Bon. But how do his wacky ideas relate to my theory of mimetic rivalry? I never refer to the racial unconscious or the crowd mind or compare rational men to children and savages. Mesmerism and hypnotism are ludicrous explanations of human social psychology.

Elias Canetti: What you get from Le Bon are your two central concepts: imitation and contagion. Le Bon takes over Tarde's "imitative instinct" and argues that it leads to crowd "contagion," what you call "mimetic contagion" or "mimetic snowballing." It is worth noting that the idea human passions could be unconsciously contagious goes back at least to the Scottish philosopher Dugald Stewart, who argued in 1827 that the "principle of sympathetic imitation," when combined with "contagious example," leads to the rapid and uncontrollable spread of hysteria within a crowd—which Stewart compares to a fever. We have already established that imitation and social contagion are two quite distinct and real phenomena. Unfortunately, social theorists from Stewart to Le Bon to our very own Girard have attempted to merge them in their explanations of crowd behavior.

René Girard: I have adopted the wider and more general concept of mimesis precisely to avoid the conflation of imitation and contagion. Desire among individuals is imitative and rivalrous. But those rivalries can themselves become contagious, leading to the crisis of violence, the war of all against all. Then, as a few people identify a plausible scapegoat, the redirection of violence onto the victim is also contagious. Alternatively, switching from a biological to a chemical metaphor, as preferred by you: a crowd crystal rapidly grows into a full-blown crowd. So desire is intrinsically imitative, but social behavior is often contagious. Hence, my theory both unites and distinguishes imitation from contagion.

Gordon Allport: René, I wish your own writings were remotely that lucid. Why are great talkers usually poor writers?

Elias Canetti: In retrospect, what is most important about the theories of Tarde and Le Bon is their assumption that the crowd is the key to understanding social life. This whole tradition of French sociology treats the crowd—sometimes implicitly and sometimes explicitly—as the paradigm of society. When we enter a crowd, we enter society and must conform to its rules, language, mores, and etiquette. The maxim "when in Rome do as the Romans" applies with special force to joining a crowd. One might say that a crowd is a miniature and more intense version of society—where there is less room, so to speak, for individuality. All societies exert pressure to conform and this pressure is especially vivid, even frightening, in a crowd. Similarly, everything that can be said about the similarities and differences among members of a crowd applies to any society. Especially in our democratic age, when the distinction between the crowd and the mass is often blurred, informal crowds are an apt symbol of the larger society. From Le Bon's "mind of the crowd" it is but a short step to Durkheim's "collective consciousness of the nation." Hence, Durkheim defined society as an organized crowd. It makes good intellectual sense to use a crowd to study social life more generally. In society, the mechanisms of conformity are subtler, more indirect, and more obscure; in a crowd, by contrast, the mechanisms of conformity are direct, obvious, and sometimes brutal.

René Girard: I see where this is going. Yes, you are right: I use the unity of the lynch mob to explain all forms of social unity. A lynch mob brings together the most diverse set of people, creating what the Americans call "strange bedfellows." No other crowd has the unanimity of a lynch mob. I am the first to agree that subsequent moments of social harmony lack the deep bonds of the shared terror and thrill experienced by the lynch mob; in our military adventures, in our rituals of capital punishment, in our religious rites, and in our blood sports, we attempt to recapture that primal unity. So yes, I belong to the tradition of inquiry that sees the crowd as the paradigm of society. Not any crowd, of course, but the lynch mob.

Elias Canetti: Actually, I would say that a crowd is an inverse image of society—society reflected in a carnival mirror. In society, we devote an immense amount of attention to policing boundaries—boundaries of personal space, of private property, of reputation, of status. At some level, we must resent all of these boundaries and all of the anxiety they produce because when we join a crowd we abandon them. From a constant fear of being touched, we are now squeezed and jostled on all sides; from desire to be distinguished from others, we now merge with others; from respect for private property, we destroy property. Crowds liberate us from the many social conventions that distance us from other people. Crowds remind us that basically we are just like everyone else—a vulnerable mammal seeking safety in the herd.

So I reject the French notion that crowds are a microcosm of society, though I agree that we can learn much about society by studying them. An equally important theme in French theories of crowds is the idea that crowds form the seedbed of all religious experience. Le Bon said that the sentiments of the crowd mind are always religious sentiments: devotion, sacrifice, worship, intolerance, fanaticism, and blind submission. The crowd, he said, always demands a god, meaning a leader. And, like religions, crowds are deeply conservative in their attachment to ritual and their fetishizing of particular objects. Tarde compared the way crowds grow to how religions proselytize, and many theorists have traced religious ecstasy to the frenzy of crowds. But it is Durkheim, of course, who devoted the greatest effort to showing that religious experience is always a by-product of "crowd effervescence." In his seminal book, *The Elementary Forms of Religious Life*, Durkheim argues that the basis of all religions is the distinction between sacred and profane objects. Well, it turns out that the realm of the sacred is co-extensive with the realm of the social. What the crowd worships as god is always itself—for compared to a single, vulnerable, and dependent individual, society is god. To a person born into it, society appears all-powerful, all-nourishing, and immortal. It is the embodiment of justice and the creator of all institutions. Individuals come and go, but society is eternal.

Durkheim studied ethnographic reports of religious ceremonies among the Australian aborigines. In these gatherings, Durkheim argued that a unique kind of electricity emerged which transported the participants into an avalanche of passion; the effervescence reached such a point of intensity that they could not be restrained. The participants reported feeling elevated and transformed into superior and higher beings. The Catholic Mass is certainly less effervescent than these rites, but Catholics share the feeling of communal elevation, of lifting the heart and mind to God. In my own theory of crowds, I see particular kinds of crowds, the small closed crowds I call "packs," as the origins of religion. There were different kinds of packs for different kinds of early religious ceremonies: "increase packs" led to fertility rituals; "lamenting packs" led to mourning rites; "hunting packs" led to sacrifice; "war packs" led to religious conquest; and "lynch packs" led to scapegoating.

Gordon Allport: Of course, if religious believers were to realize they were worshipping only themselves, what would happen to religion? I guess religion, like Girard's crowd, rests upon *méconnaissance*.

Sigmund Freud: As much as I have enjoyed this discussion, I must object to the nearly total absence of any discussion of crowds in relation to their leaders. How shall I put this delicately: there are no crowds without leaders and no leaders without crowds. A key way that a crowd is a microcosm of society is that a crowd has a leader. The two phenomena are co-extensive, and any adequate theory of crowds must also be a theory of leaders. I hasten to note that in the works of Girard and of Canetti there is very little mention of crowd leaders. One gets the impression from your theories that crowds are somehow headless, which is no more possible for a crowd than for a body, not to mention a body politic. Since leaders are always father figures, I must ask my colleagues whether they have issues with their own fathers?

Elias Canetti: I reject your dogmatic assertion that all crowds must have leaders. I myself have participated in protest crowds that were leaderless. But Theodor Adorno challenged me on this very point, and I conceded that although not all crowds have leaders, lynch mobs always have leaders. So a theory of crowd leaders is more essential to Girard's theory of the scapegoating crowd than to my comprehensive theory of crowds. The absence of a focus on crowd leaders is especially surprising in a theory of crowd imitation and crowd contagion, such as Girard's. According to Le Bon, the crowd imitates above all its leader, and the fever that possesses a crowd usually begins in the delirium of its leader. Tarde memorably described the relationship of a leader to a crowd as a madman leading sleepwalkers.

René Girard: I quite deliberately say nothing about crowd leaders. There is no viable theory of crowd leaders, who range from Saint Francis to Hitler. I suppose Max Weber would call both leaders "charismatic," but any quality that applies to both of those men must be essentially empty. Nor is it clear that leaders even lead; often leaders follow the crowd. In the immortal words of Alexandre Auguste Ledru-Rollin: "I must follow the people because I am their leader." No! Leaders come and go; they have nothing in common with each other. What remain are crowds and societies.

Sigmund Freud: I see myself very much in the tradition of French crowd theorists, so let me explain how. To begin, Tarde and Le Bon emphasized the unconscious nature of crowd psychology. Tarde, like Girard, insists that imitation stems from mechanisms that operate below the level of conscious awareness. Le Bon explicitly describes the crowd mind as the unconscious mind—that is why he compares crowds to children and to savages, both of whom have not developed adequate powers of conscious regulation of behavior. In my terms, when we join a crowd we voluntarily surrender—for a time—our ego-inhibitions. In this way, joining a crowd has the same appeal as getting drunk: we enjoy not always feeling so inhibited. Let's face it: constant self-control, self-policing, and self-censoring are exhausting. We need a break. Here there are two possibilities. First, we can join an ecstatic and orgiastic crowd, yielding our own ego to the collective unconscious of the id. We thus surrender to our base instincts of sexual pleasure, violence, and death. Or, second, we can join a disciplined crowd led by a father figure, in which case we yield our ego to his superego. Le Bon and Tarde were both quite frank about the passion for blind submission that characterizes most crowds. Crowds long to worship a leader, to obey a father. Whether we submit to the collective id or to the superego of a leader, in joining a crowd we yield our personal ego.

You might be wondering: what's libido got to do with it? In my view, the French theorists exaggerate the roles of imitation and contagion in explaining crowd solidarity. I think the primary reason we surrender our individuality when we join a crowd is love: we love our fellow travelers in a crowd, and we become a band of brothers; we also often love the leader of the crowd as a father. When we love someone, we imitate and obey him. So, yes, imitation and submission do operate in crowds but mainly because of love. We are social and familial animals: we love our fellows and our fathers.

Elias Canetti: Are crowds models of society? How do crowds relate to religion?

Sigmund Freud: I was hoping you would ask. Yes, the psychic forces that lead us to join crowds also lead us to cooperate in all other forms of social life. So, again, I follow the French theorists in seeing the crowd as the paradigm of society. And yes, again, I also see the crowd as the seedbed of all religious life. Let me preface my remarks by saying that no one should be dogmatic when speculating about human prehistory. Our speculations may be well-informed, but they remain what Kipling called "just so" stories. I follow Darwin's hypothesis of a primal horde led by an alpha-male patriarch who controls all access to the females. In this situation, the sons of the patriarch are stuck in an Oedipal dilemma: to have sex, they must kill their father and sleep with their mothers. When they do kill their father, they celebrate their liberation by eating his body. From this original murder and communal meal come all religious rituals of sacrifice and fellowship. I also follow William Robertson Smith, who argues that sacrifice is best understood as a communal meal: the person or animal is first killed and then eaten. Contemporary rituals of the Christian Eucharist share this very sequence whereby sacrificial death is followed by the fellowship of the communal meal of the body and blood. Through these rituals we commemorate the primal killing of the father, which sexually liberated his sons so that they could create their own families and other societies. This original murder is the origin simultaneously of society and of religion.

René Girard: Perhaps I have suppressed my debts to Tarde and Le Bon, but I certainly have never failed to acknowledge my debt to Freud's great *Totem and Taboo*. I also trace all religious rites to sacrifice and all sacrifice to an original murder. But in my story the sons do not murder their fathers; rather, the primal horde, to escape its own crisis of internal rivalry, learns to select an arbitrary victim and to kill it. The death of the surrogate-victim creates such an overwhelming experience of unity and harmony that the horde continues to commemorate this original murder in rituals of sacrifice, at first with human victims and then with animals. In these ritual sacrifices, an animal is selected by a priest representing the whole people. Often, the priest then transfers the sins of the people upon the sacrificial victim, just as the destructive mimetic rivalry of the horde was originally transferred upon the surrogate-victim. The crowd then witnesses the sacrificial killing, remembers the salutary death of the scapegoat, and recreates the primal harmony by a ritual meal of communal fellowship. Obviously, I consider my theory superior to Freud's because my theory of mimetic desire is superior to his theory of individual libido. But our theories of the crowd origins of religion are of the same general type, and so I do not want to indulge in what my friend Sigmund rightly calls the narcissism of minor difference.

Elias Canetti: I hate to question this generous gesture of reconciliation, but in terms of your basic theoretical logics I am afraid, René, that you and Freud are fundamentally opposed. There are only a few possible kinds of explanations of the relation between individual and crowd behavior. Plato represents one possibility: the crowd is simply the individual writ large. Meanwhile, Tarde and Le Bon give classic expression to the contagion theory: the individual adopts the mind of the crowd (and/or its leader) by a process of unconscious imitation and emotional contagion. Durkheim is also committed to this general type of explanation, though it only comes out clearly in his discussion of "crowd effervescence." Freud, by contrast, offers a totally different explanation for why the individual conforms to the crowd: each person independently desires to surrender his ego-inhibitions to the crowd. In this way, the crowd does not mesmerize the individual; rather, each individual independently converges on the crowd. Because each person is a locus of his own libidinal energies, he can choose to cathect these energies on the crowd and its leader. René, despite your generous overtures to Sigmund, your own theory is clearly of the contagion-type. Individuals, on your account, do not independently converge upon the crowd; rather, mimetic snowballing leads them, willy-nilly, into it. Hence, as I said before, Girard belongs squarely in the French tradition of crowd-contagion theorists, despite the fact that he and his commentators talk endlessly about Freud and never mention Tarde or Le Bon. Freud, however, is the leading "convergence" theorist of crowds. The final approach to explaining how individuals relate to crowds could be called "interactional." This approach, championed by Talcott Parsons and his followers, sees crowd behavior as the by-product of the many face-to-face negotiations made by its members. In this view, crowd norms and actions are the evolving product of the many individual interactions among crowd participants and leaders.

Gordon Allport: What I like most about Freud's theory of collective psychology is his first-person perspective: he tells us why an individual might be motivated to join a crowd. In the same way, I attempted to offer a first-person perspective on why someone might be tempted to find a scapegoat. I find all this talk about hypnosis, contagion, and a "crowd mind" to be bizarre.

Elias Canetti: I also offer a first-person perspective on crowds in my book, *Crowds and Power*. In fact, I am the only person here who has actually participated in large crowd demonstrations. It is curious that the major theorists of crowds—Plato, Nietzsche, Tarde, Le Bon, Durkheim, Freud, and Girard—all suffer from enochlophobia, the fear of crowds. I wonder if, by extension, all major social theorists are recluses or misanthropes.

Gordon Allport: Yes, but on your account, people are motivated to join crowds because they want to get over their fear of being touched. Surely this cannot be a dominant motivation. Let's pose this question: Why would a rational individual choose to join a crowd? All social theory should develop its fundamental distinctions and categories in relation to the practical reasoning of a mature and conscientious person. No doubt there are some crowds that we would not choose to join, such as panic or flight crowds. But there are other crowds that we would choose to join, including crowds of pilgrims as well as protest crowds. Despite Canetti's exhaustive and exhausting classification of crowds, he fails to make this elementary distinction between voluntary and involuntary crowds.

It seems to me quite rational for an ordinary citizen to join a protest crowd or demonstration: he or she does not need to be seduced, hypnotized, or subjected to passionate contagion. Every protestor understands that his or her voice will be effective only if magnified, amplified, and multiplied by the voice of a crowd. In all modern societies, democratic or not, numbers matter: even perfectly peaceful but truly immense and patient crowds can bring down long-standing autocratic regimes, as we saw throughout Central and Eastern Europe in 1989. The people have the ultimate political power—if only they will assemble as a crowd. After all, if autocratic governments reject the voice of the people, can they dissolve the people and elect a new people?

True, if we interpret individual rationality too narrowly, as do the economists, then paradoxes emerge as each person realizes that his or her presence in a large crowd is of little consequence and is perhaps not worth the effort. But fortunately most of us are rational in a broader sense and see the value of expressing our views in public with our fellow citizens. And even a few people who take a stand can become "crowd crystals," using Canetti's helpful image. I am astounded that these very simple observations about the rationality of joining political crowds are totally absent from high theorizing about crowds.

Sigmund Freud: Gordon, I agree with what you say. But your focus on individual rationality only goes so far in explaining the depths of human motivation. I want to argue that Canetti's analysis of crowd symbols gives us a key to understanding some of the deepest sources of the magnetic pull of the crowd. What are the main symbols or metaphors we use to describe crowds? Canetti lists, among others, fire, the sea, rivers, the forest, wind, and sand. What these symbols have in common is that in addition to being symbols of crowds, they are also examples of the sublime. Recall that Burke defined the experience of the sublime in terms of uncontrollable danger, the unbounded infinite, and dark power. What is less controllable than the wind, fire, or the sea? What is more unbounded than the wind, the sea, or the sand? What is more obscurely immense than the sea or the forest? What is more dangerous than a river, fire, or the wind? Immanuel Kant distinguishes the mathematical from the dynamical sublime. The mathematical sublime refers to the awe-inspiring sight of an innumerable mass of identical elements, as in a vast array of columns, the starry sky, the sand on a beach, or trees in a forest. The dynamical sublime refers to the terrifying experience of sensing an immensely powerful, moving, unbounded, and undifferentiated mass, such as the ocean or the wind. I know of no phenomenon exemplifying both the mathematical and the dynamical sublime besides large crowds. When static, huge crowds are awe-inspiring masses of innumerable and identical elements, like a forest or the starry sky; when moving, the same crowds become truly terrifying—all-powerful, unbounded, uncontrollable, and undifferentiated, like a raging river, a fiery conflagration, or a swelling ocean. What could be more sublime and awful than a forest in motion, a myriad of columns on the march, a galaxy of stars swirling? Despite its terrors, we are attracted to the sublime; we long to escape the narrow confines of our individual lives and to belong to something much larger. The crowd is both terrifying and comforting; there is both danger and safety in numbers. This profound experience of the sublime in the midst of a crowd helps to explain not only its irresistible attraction but also its inescapable religious dimension. The immensity, the power, and the danger of a crowd point us to the divine Godhead, who often reveals himself in the guise of a crowd symbol, such as fire or a storm.

CHAPTER FIVE

Scapegoating Sacrifice: A Discussion Moderated by John Milbank

John Milbank: It is a delight to bring together René Girard and a set of experts on the theory and practice of sacrifice. Joseph de Maistre is the first writer to argue that sacrifice is the basis of all social order; Maistre sees all political violence in terms of ritual slaughter and atonement. Rabbi Jacob Milgrom has written the authoritative twentieth-century commentary on the sacrificial rituals of the Hebrew Bible. And Father Robert J. Daly, S.J., has written authoritative studies about the meaning of sacrifice in the Christian Bible and in Christian theology. These men are well situated to evaluate Girard's provocative claims. We meet, of course, in view of Jerusalem's Temple Mount, the site of so much sacrificial killing, both ancient and modern. Despite the biblical condemnation of human sacrifice, countless human beings, Jewish, Christian, and Muslim, have been sacrificed here in God's name.

Girard is certainly not alone among nineteenth- and twentieth-century anthropologists who argue that sacrifice is at the foundation of all human religious ritual. Virtually every known human culture originally practiced human and later animal sacrifice. What this means is that for thousands of years, all over the earth human beings devoted immense labor, time, and resources to the ritual slaughter of millions of human and animal victims. What is the meaning of this universal and infinite ritual slaughter? Why is it that wherever we find human beings, we find rivers of sacrificial bloodletting? How does all this ritual violence relate to other kinds of horrific violence in murder and in war? It is tempting to avert our eyes from the awful spectacle of ritual sacrifice—the cutting of throats, the hacking of bones, the evisceration of organs, the screams, the oceans of smoking blood, and the immolation of victims. Archaeologists keep discovering the hecatombs of human and animal bones, scarred by the blades of ritual slaughter. Often they find the remains of children sacrificed by their parents. Girard refuses to look away: he is convinced that this immense project of ritual violence holds the key to understanding human religion and human social order. For Girard, it is no accident that the Nazi genocide is described in terms of ritual sacrifice, for the Holocaust can be understood only in reference to religious holocausts.

René Girard: We so easily forget the fragility of human social order. Mimetic rivalry, envy, spite, and fear lurk everywhere, waiting to escalate into catastrophic violence. All that holds murder at bay, at least temporarily, is sacrifice. The need to kill our rival is so urgent that it cannot be simply suppressed. This violence can only be redirected: first from our neighbors onto scapegoats and then from scapegoats onto human and animal sacrificial victims. Religions arose to ritualize, control, and sublimate human violence. They do so by means of a twofold substitution: the scapegoat as a substitute for random communal violence and then the sacrificial victim as a substitute for the scapegoat. These substitutions form the basis of all human culture, since human thought and language rests upon the substitution of one thing for another—a word for a concept or a symbol for a thing. Hence, sacrificial substitution, in which the victim symbolizes the scapegoat, is the basis for the whole of human linguistic and cultural achievement.

Unlike naïve utopians from Plato to the present, priests have always understood that violence is inescapable in human life and must be administered in medicinal doses. Jesus was certainly not naïve about violence when he said: "Only Satan can cast out Satan." Only sacred violence can control profane violence. Homeopathic violence is the only remedy for catastrophic violence. Those who think that we have escaped these primitive urges need only consider the enormous popularity of blood sports, violent video games, capital punishment, and war today. The governments of the most powerful nations on earth are preparing daily for the eventual and inevitable nuclear holocaust—the ultimate immolation, and the final sacrifice.

John Milbank: Is there any escape from this horrible machinery of endless sacrifice? Must there always be scapegoats and sacrificial victims?

René Girard: Yes, there is an escape but only through a universal and radical conversion to Christian pacifism. When God incarnate became the sacrificial victim at Calvary, He marked the end of the age of sacrifice. Jesus came into the world for no other reason than to bring an end to mimetic rivalry, scapegoating, and sacrifice. How could He do this more clearly than by Himself becoming the victim of a scapegoating murder? In my view, Jesus's critique of sacrifice is already foreshadowed in the Old Testament, especially in the prophets. Christianity is the enemy of all religion because religion rests upon sacrificial killing.

John Milbank: Well, I guess Nietzsche was right when he said that the last Christian died upon the cross. First, Christians themselves have been enthusiastic scapegoaters of Jews, Muslims, and heretics. Second, Christians continue the cult of sacrifice in the form of the Eucharistic sacrifice of the Mass. Third, the ancient logic of sacrificial substitution is the basis of the traditional medieval theology of vicarious atonement through penal substitution, such as we find in Saint Anselm. According to this theology, Jesus received the punishment that all of us deserved; he was the innocent lamb sacrificed on our behalf. Most Christians still affirm this doctrine of penal substitution. How is this redirection of violence different from the ancient religions you disparage?

René Girard: I should have said: Jesus announced the end of scapegoating and of sacrificial violence. Clearly, the world was not yet ready to hear His message. Judging from how my own exposition of the evangelical critique of violence has been received, I doubt the world will ever be ready to hear His message. Jesus's own death as revealed to us in the Gospels has no connection to ritual sacrifice, despite many influential interpretations to the contrary.

Joseph de Maistre: Girard and his commentators virtually never mention my name, yet Girard falls squarely in the French tradition of thought about sacrifice and politics that began with me. I was the first theorist to argue that there is no society where there is no sacrifice. Ancient society was possible because of the priestly sacrificer; modern society is possible because of the executioner. And there is no religious ritual in which blood does not play a part. Back in the early nineteenth century, I predicted that ancient holocausts would culminate in a modern Holocaust: "The entire earth, continually steeped in blood, is naught but an immense altar where all that lives must be immolated, without end, without measure, without pause, until the consummation of things, the extinction of evil, unto the death of death." I pioneered Durkheim's and Girard's functional analysis of religion by arguing that there cannot be a false religion because every religion serves the same sacrificial function.

Thomas Jefferson famously said: "I tremble for my country when I reflect that God is just, that His justice will not sleep forever." Here Jefferson, not usually a perceptive student of religion, captures the fundamental quandary of the religious mind. We are conscious both of our own iniquity and of the goodness of the gods; we know that we deserve to be punished, so we attempt to propitiate the gods by substituting another victim in our place. The basic principle for this substitution is an innocent life for a guilty one, so we offer innocent children and innocent animals to be killed in our place. One soul for another soul—the ancients called this *antipsychōn* or *vicariam animam*—a substitute soul. Men live under the hand of an irritated power, and this power can be appeased only by blood sacrifices. From this logic of the substitution of expiatory suffering men were led to the dreadful practice of human sacrifice. When our ancestors began to substitute animals for humans, notice that they chose the most human-like domesticated animals as victims. Why does no culture sacrifice wild animals?

What truth cannot be found in paganism? Pagans recognized that all redemption comes from sacrifice, a truth that was once and for all consummated by the sacrifice of Jesus for the redemption of mankind.

René Girard: Joseph, rest assured: I admire you very much. However, thanks to Isaiah Berlin, you are widely regarded today as a proto-fascist. To praise you in public is to invite calumny. But here I am happy to honor you as the first modern person to see that violence is the origin of religion and to see that sacrifice is the foundation of social order. In a world of naïve Enlightenment liberals, you remind us of the inescapable horrors of the human condition. You are also right about the centrality of substitution, but in your theory the innocent victim is substituted for the guilty sacrificer, whereas in my theory the surrogate-victim is substituted for the whole community. I reject your moralizing theory of substitution: I don't see communities as being so morally squeamish—any victim will do. In short, you do not see that the scapegoat gives us the key to understanding sacrifice. Finally, you stress the continuity between Christian and pagan sacrifice while I insist that Christianity rejects sacrificial violence once and for all. By the way, I have been meaning to tell you that you write French more beautifully than anyone in history who never lived in France. *Le style, c'est l'homme!*

Joseph de Maistre: Thank you for that long-overdue encomium. One can receive no better education in the violent, bloody horror of human life than by living in Saint Petersburg. As for Christianity and paganism, despite some of my rhetorical flourishes I do see some important differences. To Voltaire's infamous claim that the "sacrifices" (*sic*) of the Inquisition were a hundred times worse than ordinary pagan human sacrifice ("we have substituted executioners for butchers"), I retorted that were it not for Christianity, parents would still be offering their children by the thousands into the maw of Moloch. So, yes, Christianity does represent immense moral progress despite the ignorant protests of the shallow *philosophes* to the contrary. But Christianity also teaches that "without the shedding of blood, there is no forgiveness of sins" (Hebrews 9:22). True, we have abolished human and animal sacrifice, but we continue to honor the sacrifices of the martyrs and saints whose innocent blood redeems the world. Who can deny its efficacy? Louis XVI and Marie Antoinette were innocent sacrificial victims offered to expiate the sins of the

Revolution, just as the Romanovs were sacrificed by the Bolsheviks to atone for the sins of Russia. Sacrifice ranges from the lowest horrors of Moloch to the highest expression of Christian love in the self-sacrifice of the saints for the salvation of the world. There is no society without self-sacrifice.

John Milbank: One is reluctant to agree with Maistre, who seems to celebrate—not just describe—human violence, but agree we must. The Holocaust has forever changed the way we view biblical holocausts. When Aaron, the first high priest in the Bible, slaughters and then immolates innocent lambs in a fiery sacrifice, how can we not think of Nazi crematoria? Indeed, the German killing of innocent civilians during that war more closely resembles a sacrificial rite than the contest of a battle. Just like ritual sacrifice, German killing was orderly, methodical, and efficient. There was virtually no resistance or unseemly conflict. Jews herded into German camps were often described as "lambs going to the slaughter," so it is no accident that the Nazi genocide was soon dubbed a "Holocaust"—that is, a sacrificial killing of biblical proportions. In short, the Nazis gave all methodical killing, including sacrificial rites, a bad name.

René Girard: The key to understanding sacrifice in the original sense is understanding the scapegoat ritual. In many if not all ancient cultures we find a ritual in which a person or an animal is selected (called a *pharmakos* in Greek or a "go-away goat" in the Bible); then the community or a priest representing the community transfers the evils of that community onto the scapegoat; finally, the scapegoat is expelled from the community. My argument is that this ritual reveals the secret of all sacrifices: the sins of the community are transferred onto a surrogate, and the surrogate is expelled or killed. Social harmony can be sustained only if the community is able to redirect its internal violent conflicts onto a suitable victim. Our best description of this ancient ritual can be found in the Bible (Leviticus 16:7–22). Aaron presents two goats to the Lord. Aaron then casts lots and one goat is sacrificed to the Lord while the other goat (the scapegoat) is sent away into the wilderness to Azazel, a demon. Before the scapegoat is sent away, Aaron places both of his hands on the head of the live goat and transfers all the sins of Israel onto the goat. Here we can see the close connection to the modern sense of scapegoating: the collective sins (violence) of the many are transferred to the single victim, who is then expelled (or worse). In short, our modern notion of a scapegoat clearly derives from this biblical ritual. Moreover, by setting the two goats together before the Lord, Aaron is clearly showing us the close relation between the scapegoat and the sacrificial goat as well as between scapegoating and sacrifice, both of which involve the use of surrogate victims to expiate the sins of the community.

Jacob Milgrom: The phenomenon of social-psychological "scapegoating," which involves persecution and violent abuse, obviously has no relationship whatsoever to the biblical scapegoat. As Mary Douglas and others have pointed out, the "go-away goat" is not subjected to any violence, not even humiliation or contempt.

I wish to address Girard's more important claim that the scapegoat ritual explains the origins and nature of sacrifice. According to Girard, the scapegoat is a substitute for the community, a surrogate victim. Rather than punish Israel, the Most High punishes the scapegoat. Similarly, says Girard, when a person brings an offering to the altar to be sacrificed, he transfers his sin to the animal, which is then killed in place of the sinner. Since the sins of the people are explicitly transferred by Aaron to the scapegoat, are not sins transferred to every offering? Is not every sacrifice the killing of a surrogate-victim? These are profound questions to ask about biblical rituals.

Let me first explain why the scapegoat ritual has nothing to do with sacrifice, and then I'll explain why the scapegoat is not a surrogate-victim for Israel. First, the goat sent to Azazel is not an offering of any kind; it is not treated as a sacrifice, which requires slaughter and blood manipulation. Moreover, an animal laden with impurities would not be an acceptable offering either to the Holy One or to a demon. Second, the goat is not a surrogate-victim for Israel because there is no indication that the goat is punished or demonically attacked in Israel's place. Neither is Azazel thought to be discharging his work on Israel nor has Israel offended Azazel: there is no prayer to Azazel to make him act in a beneficent manner or to receive the goat as a substitute. Instead of being an offering or substitute, the goat is simply a vehicle to dispatch Israel's impurities and sins to the wilderness or netherworld—returning them whence they came.

Robert Daly: Yes, Jacob is certainly right here: the scapegoat ritual is neither a sin-offering nor a sacrifice.

René Girard: Of course the scapegoat is a sacrifice! In both rituals, the priest lays his hands on the animal to transfer the community's sins onto it; then both animals are punished for the sins. That is the definition of a surrogate-victim. Being expelled from the community to almost certain death in the wilderness—how is this not a punishment? Who can fail to see the close parallels between these two goats? Thomas Hobbes pointed out that the Leviticus ritual was a figure for the suffering of Jesus, who was both the scapegoat and the sacrificed goat, again showing the close connection between the two goats.

Jacob Milgrom: I am delighted that you referred to the hand-laying ritual since it is so often misunderstood, especially by Christians. In the scapegoat ritual, Aaron places both hands on the goat. The fact that the text stresses that the hand-laying rite is executed with both hands is the key to understanding the function of the Azazel goat. It is not a sacrifice, else the hand-laying would have been performed with one hand. All sacrifices involve the laying on of only one hand. As for Hobbes, even if Jesus did suffer the fate of both Levictical goats, this in no way implies a similarity between scapegoating and sacrifice.

René Girard: Now you are getting my goat! Are you saying that the same ritual cannot be performed with one or with two hands?

Jacob Milgrom: Once I explain the nature of biblical sacrifice, you'll understand why even the tiniest variations in ritual are supremely important. Here my purpose is only to explain why the scapegoat ritual has nothing to do with sacrifice. To understand the scapegoat, we must look to a very different ritual: the cleansing of leprosy (Leviticus 14:1–8).

Here the priest is brought two birds. One of the birds is killed, and its blood is sprinkled over a man who is to be cleansed of leprosy and sprinkled over the live bird. Then the priest pronounces the man cleansed and immediately releases the live bird into an open field. Sin is often compared to disease in the Bible, so these two rituals involve the cleansing of sin by transferring it to animals which then escape. The go-away goat parallels not the sacrificed goat but the go-away bird. I realize that putting the scapegoat in the context of curing leprosy lacks the dramatic violence of Girard's surrogate-victim, but I am interested in explaining the Bible, not human violence.

René Girard: In my view, you have whitewashed the callous cruelty of expelling the scapegoat into the wilderness. The key to the scapegoat is not found in the ritual of the cleansing of leprosy but in the ritual punishment of blasphemy in Leviticus 24:13–14. Here the whole people of Israel place their hands (plural) upon the blasphemer before stoning him. Just as Aaron transferred the sins of Israel upon the goat by placing his hands upon it, so here the whole people transfer their sins upon the blasphemer before killing him. Clearly, the blasphemer, like the goat, is a surrogate victim.

But even if violence in scapegoat rituals is not dramatic or bloody, violence is certainly front and center in rituals of sacrifice. Here innocent animals—birds, lambs, goats, and calves—have their throats slit, and while they are still living, their blood drained from their bodies. Then they are hacked to pieces, and all the organs are removed; some parts of the animal are to be eaten, while other parts are to be immolated by fire on the altar. No decent person could witness this violence without a shudder. The innocent animals are murdered by the priests, who are blood-soaked murderers. These awful rituals are performed every day in the Temple, meaning that over the centuries the Levitical priests have killed millions of animals. How can one explain this orgy of violence? It can only be explained by my theory of the surrogate-victim mechanism. We murder the animal to redirect the violence that once threatened the whole society. In sacrifice, we commemorate and recreate the harmony achieved by the original scapegoat murder. Sacrificial violence is the remedy for social violence.

John Milbank: Levitical priests are murderers? I guess I don't see why humanely killing animals counts as murder. In agricultural and pastoral societies most animals are routinely killed anyway—so why is sacrificial killing especially awful? How ironic that those who claim to be horrified by ancient sacrifice never voice any protest over the much crueler abuse and torture of animals in modern factory farming. I submit that these ancient holocausts are shocking only if seen in light of the modern Holocaust. It was only after the Second World War that scholars such as Girard and Walter Burkert began to see ancient sacrifice as a harbinger of modern human violence. Perhaps we are scapegoating sacrifice.

Moreover, I don't see why you are condemning sacrifice at all since you see it as curative and preventative of much worse violence. Shouldn't you be praising the priests for their noble work in redirecting human violence onto animals?

Joseph de Maistre: Girard and I did not need the Holocaust to understand the social function of sacrifice. We had Robespierre and the Terror. Both of us frequently refer to the executions of Louis XVI and his queen as paradigms of sacrificial killing. In my reading, God permitted the deaths of the innocent monarchs as a substitute for all the guilty revolutionaries. The king and queen nobly accepted the punishment that the crowd deserved. In this way, God's justice was satisfied by vicarious atonement. In Girard's reading, the crowd selected the royals to be scapegoats, blaming them for the crisis of violence unleashed by the revolution. In the theatrical spectacle, the crowd was engulfed in a frenzy of blood, death, dismemberment, and revenge. The crisis of violence was over and the crowd enjoyed at least a temporary peace and harmony.

Jacob Milgrom: If we hope to understand biblical sacrifice, we must consider how the ancient priests themselves understood sacrifice. For this we need to turn away from Maistre and other theorists of violence and turn instead to Marcel Mauss's essay *The Gift*. Let's begin with the language of the Hebrew Bible. Our word "sacrifice" stems from the Latin word meaning "to make holy"; but in English "sacrifice" strongly connotes killing and death. The Bible speaks not of sacrifices but of offerings (*korban*, or in the Greek Bible, *dōron*). What is an offering? As Moshe Halbertal nicely explains, an offering is a special kind of gift. Normally, when giving a gift to a peer or social inferior, we can expect our gift to be received. But when giving a gift to a superior, especially to the Most High, we cannot assume that our gift will be accepted. Hence, we do not presume to "give" a gift to the Holy One but merely "offer" a gift to Him. Because we hope that our offering will be accepted, we follow precise and divinely ordained rituals to ensure that our gift will be pleasing to the Holy One. What you misleadingly call "sacrifice," then, is the transference of property from the profane to the sacred realm. The Hebrew word *'ola*, which is the basis of the Greek word *holocaust*, means "that which ascends," implying that the offering is entirely turned to smoke. Why is the offering turned to smoke? Does this imply the violence of annihilation?

Robert Daly: Not at all. The only way to give a physical gift to a spiritual being is to sublimate it into a spiritual form. By consuming the gift completely in fire, the smoke rises to Heaven where, according to the Bible, God can savor the smell. Yes, the whole ritual of the burnt offering makes sense only as a solution to the problem of transmitting a physical gift to a spiritual being. The Hebrews were certainly not alone in arriving at this solution: virtually every human culture burns its offerings to the gods. Sacrifices are kinds of gifts not kinds of violence.

Jacob Milgrom: The burnt offering is a gift, and gifts are given, naturally, for a variety of motives: homage, thanksgiving, appeasement, expiation, and so on. If biblical offerings were about violence they would be structured very differently. To begin with, most burnt offerings were not of animals at all. The *minchah* was the "poor man's burnt offering" of grain, bread, wine, and oil. Because most Hebrews could not afford to offer animals, the most frequent burnt offerings were the cereal offerings (Leviticus 24:5–9). The cereal offerings were in no way subsidiary or of lesser covenantal effect than the animal offerings. In fact, cereal cakes were in some ways even more central to Temple practice than were animal offerings. One would never guess from Girard's lurid language that most biblical sacrifices involved the killing and the immolating of cakes of cereal!

As for animal offerings, even here the biblical rituals lack all violent drama. The Romans, for example, were experts in the use of theatrical violence for the purpose of public edification. Roman spectacles involved the violent slaying of wild animals or of armed men because these kinds of killing involved a struggle and conflict, which is the essence of violence. Biblical rituals, by contrast, always involved only domesticated animals, ensuring no conflict or drama. It is significant that only male animals were eligible for a holocaust because virtually all male animals in agricultural societies were killed when very young anyway; hence, the ritual offering merely turned necessity into a virtue.

Robert Daly: Yes, and although Girard strongly emphasizes the essential role of blood in sacrifice, it is important to note that the blood-rite was ritually distinct from the rite of burnt offering—so, strictly speaking, blood played no role whatever in sacrifice proper. The quasi-Girardian idea expressed in Hebrews that "without the shedding of blood, there is no forgiveness of sins" is clearly false in view of the centrality of the burnt cereal offerings. Atonement was commonly sought without any blood.

John Milbank: Whether violent or not, aren't all these gift offerings just a way to bribe God? As Mauss says in *The Gift*, the maxim of the gift relation is "I give so that you will give" (*do ut des*). I find it very objectionable to relate to God by offering Him bribes so that He will not kill us or so that He will bless us in return. What a crudely economic understanding of our relationship to God!

Jacob Milgrom: You are right that all gifts are exchanges, but you misinterpret the meaning of biblical offerings. Everything created was given to man as a gift from the Holy One. Hence, ritual offerings were clearly understood as expressing thanksgiving and gratitude by returning a tiny portion of what He so generously gave to us. This is the meaning of the biblical law that all firstborn males and first fruits belong to the Holy One. Burnt offerings are not a bribe but a thank-you gift.

Robert Daly: Since we are on the topic of profound theological misunderstandings of biblical sacrifice, I want to address a long-standing Christian misunderstanding. Here I refer to a particular theory of vicarious atonement which was classically articulated by Saint Anselm and known as the "penal substitution" theory of atonement. According to this theory of sacrifice, a Hebrew sinner brings his animal to the altar of the Temple and then lays his hands upon the animal's head while the priest prays that the sins of the donor be transferred to the animal. Then the priest kills the animal and annihilates it by fire. Here the Hebrew sinner seeks to deflect the punishment he deserves by substituting an animal in his place. By transferring his sin to the animal and then inflicting capital punishment on the animal, the sinner has now satisfied God's demand for justice. Justice, after all, requires only that debts be paid; justice does not require that debts always be paid by a particular person. Just as the government is satisfied if someone else pays your taxes on your behalf, so God is satisfied so long as someone or something has paid your debts by being punished on your behalf. The penal substitution view of sacrifice is focused on the death of the victim since "without the shedding of blood, there is no forgiveness of sins." Unfortunately, this interpretation of Hebrew sacrifice led to Anselm's interpretation of the meaning of the passion of Jesus. We are all guilty before God and deserve to die for our sins. Jesus, the lamb of God, offers to pay the debt we all owe by accepting capital punishment on our behalf. The shedding of his blood, then, effects our salvation by penal substitution.

I think it should be clear that Girard's theory of the "surrogate-victim" is just one variant of this general theology of penal substitution. What counts for him is that the victim is killed on behalf of all of us: whether the original scapegoat or the sacrificial offering, the victim is killed for the benefit of the whole society. Whereas the theology of penal substitution is aimed at harmony between God and man, Girard's social theory of the surrogate-victim is aimed at harmony among men.

It would take us too far afield to explore all the theological objections to the penal substitution theory of atonement. This theory, with its angry, vengeful God, strongly appeals to both conservative Christians and to atheists. But since this theory rests upon an interpretation of biblical sacrifice, it is worth considering whether it fits with the biblical texts. I submit that penal substitution is not consistent with biblical sacrifice. To begin with, biblical sacrifice does not involve punishment. One wonders how cereal cakes could be punished. Even animals are killed humanely with a minimum of pain. The death of the victim is obviously the point of capital punishment, but the point of biblical sacrifice is to make a gift to God. Yes, animals are killed, but their deaths are merely a necessary prerequisite for bringing the gift to God. Animals cannot be made acceptable to God until they are consumed by fire. No ritual significance is attached to the death of the animal; its death, in itself, effects nothing. Leviticus, in fact, says almost nothing about how to kill the animals. Thus, theories of penal substitution, in which suffering and death effect atonement, are totally without scriptural foundation.

Jacob Milgrom: Many people confuse the scapegoat ritual, in which sins are transferred to the animal, with the burnt offering, in which sins are never transferred to the animal. As I mentioned before, in burnt offering only one hand is placed on the animal, while two hands are placed on the scapegoat. Because we cannot assume that our offerings will be acceptable to the Most High, it is imperative that they be performed in precisely the right way. Hence, the distinction between the one and the two hands itself eliminates the possibility of transference in the case of burnt offerings. If the laying of one hand upon the offering is not meant to transfer sin, then what is its meaning? The donor places his hand on the animal to identify the offering as coming from him. When we give a gift to the Holy One, we want Him to know whose gift it is—it is that simple. The donor wants to rectify his relation to the Holy One by means of his gift, so it is essential that the gift be credited to the right person. In any event, the atonement possible from burnt offerings only includes inadvertent sins, not deliberate sins. Sins committed in ignorance do not deserve death; therefore there is no need for the animal to die in place of the sinner. Finally, the transfer of one's sins to the burnt offering would by definition render that offering ritually unclean and, thus, not suitable as a gift to the Holy One. These are just some of the reasons why penal substitution or vicarious atonement theories have no basis in biblical sacrifice.

John Milbank: Penal substitution or vicarious atonement may be a poor interpretation of biblical offerings, but how can we understand the Suffering Servant of Isaiah apart from these ideas? According to Isaiah, this Messianic figure was punished for our transgressions: "by his bruises we are healed" (Isaiah 53:5). So the idea of penal substitution is not totally absent from Scripture.

René Girard: Thank you, John, for mentioning Isaiah, whom I will discuss in a moment. But first I want to say that I have enjoyed learning about how the authors of the Bible understood sacrifice, just as I have enjoyed reading anthropo-logical accounts of sacrifice from many other cultures. Every culture has its own understanding of sacrifice. Some see it as a gift to the deity; others see it as a communal meal with the deity; still others see it as propitiating divine wrath. I seek a universal theory of sacrifice; you have offered me only one particular theory. Recall that on my account sacrifice, like scapegoating, rests upon *méconnaissance*, or misunderstand-ing. If the sacrificers were aware of the surrogate-victim mech-anism, then their killing would be revealed as arbitrary, and it could not fulfill its social function. If we are to provide a universal and objective theory of sacrifice, then we cannot trust the self-understanding of the sacrificers, which is irrele-vant to the objective social function of sacrifice.

More importantly, your gift theory of biblical sacrifice is not remotely consistent with the violent denunciations of sacrifice among the Hebrew prophets and in the Gospels. The whole point of the Bible—especially the Christian Bible—is to condemn sacrifice and the whole violent culture of surrogate victims. If sacrifice were as innocent as gift giving, then why would Isaiah say: "Whoever slaughters an ox is like one who kills a human being; whoever sacrifices a lamb, like one who breaks a dog's neck" (66:3; cf. 1:11)? Or why would Hosea say:

"For I desire steadfast love and not sacrifice, the knowledge of God rather than burnt offerings" (6:6)? Hosea's critique is explicitly quoted and endorsed by Jesus (Matthew 9:13; cf. 12:7). Why would Jesus cleanse the Temple if not to abolish the cult of sacrifice? According to Hebrews, Jesus's death puts an end to all sacrifice, which it says was never able to effect atonement (10:4). Every ancient religion practiced sacrifice; what makes the Bible unique is its critique and rejection of sacrifice. Again, I repeat: Christianity is the enemy of all religion because religion rests upon scapegoat killing.

John Milbank: I'll let the biblical scholars address your view that the Bible rejects sacrifice. But even if the Bible does reject sacrifice, this does not make the Bible unique, as you claim. Lucien Scubla and other classical scholars have pointed out that there are Orphic, Stoic, and other philosophical critiques of sacrifice in the ancient world that are totally independent of biblical revelation. If so, what makes the Bible unique?

René Girard: Christianity alone makes God Incarnate the victim of a scapegoating murder. What more powerful revelation of the sinister nature of the surrogate-victim mechanism could there be? Moreover, the other ancient critiques of sacrifice were not as independent of all biblical influence as some scholars claim.

Jacob Milgrom: Girard is right that there is more to the Hebrew Bible than the priestly traditions of Leviticus. The tension between prophetic and priestly religion runs throughout the Bible. Yes, the prophets strongly condemn aspects of the priestly ritual—but which aspects? It is a fundamental principle of biblical interpretation to construe texts in a way that makes the whole Bible as coherent as possible. Priestly ritual, while essential to our covenant with the Holy One, is always in danger of becoming, well, ritualistic—that is, purely formal and mechanical. One can fulfill the letter of the law without committing one's whole heart and mind to the love and service of the Most High. The prophets always insist that we owe God not just our tithes and our Temple offerings but our whole selves; the prophets warn us that simply doing our duty from habit or fear is not adequate. Prophetic critique comes from within a priestly culture and must be understood as a corrective and not as an alternative to that culture. The prophets use all the technical terms from the priestly codes; their critique takes the Temple cult for granted and aims to purify it. Ritual offerings are necessary but far from sufficient. We owe the Most High our sincere and total love and service— not simply lip service. Temple offerings can certainly degenerate into a crude economic exchange with the Holy One. The prophets rightly denounce this misunderstanding of the true purpose of the burnt offerings. Finally, if the prophets really had condemned Temple offerings root and branch, then it is difficult to explain the return of the priestly cult of burnt offerings in the post-exilic period.

Robert Daly: Girard is also right that we cannot understand Jesus's critique of Temple sacrifice without understanding the prophets. Like the Hebrew prophets, Jesus takes the system of Temple offerings for granted but also offers important correctives (Mark 1:44; 12:41f.; 7:11). For example, Jesus tells us to reconcile with our brother before leaving our gift at the altar (Matthew 5:23f.), meaning that we must work for reconciliation ourselves and not use gifts as a "magical" substitute for right conduct. To say that God prefers a clean and merciful heart to burnt offerings in no way disparages sacrifice. It just subordinates the ritual gift to the more basic gift of our own selves to God. Jesus cleanses the Temple of the money changers, who make an economic mockery of sacred rituals; Jesus's zeal for his Father's house reflects his respect for the cult, not his contempt. Yes, Jesus also radicalizes the prophetic critique when he identifies the Temple with his own body: "something greater than the Temple is here" (Matthew 12:6). When the Temple becomes the Body of Christ, then temple sacrifice becomes the self-sacrifice of all Christians for the glory of God. The prophets told us to give sacrifices of praise, thanksgiving, and deeds of mercy. Paul says that we must become "living sacrifices." In Christian self-sacrifice, not only are the internal dispositions of the person of central importance, but these dispositions are also fleshed out and externalized in ministerial deeds of preaching, healing, and forgiving.

René Girard: I see the beginning of the biblical critique of sacrifice already in the story of the sacrifice of Isaac (Genesis 22). God commands Abraham to offer his only son, Isaac, as a burnt offering. At a time when all ancient religions were practicing human sacrifice, the Bible alone offers a dramatic critique of human sacrifice when, at the last minute, God spares Isaac from Abraham's knife and substitutes a ram for Isaac. Here we also see a revelation of the truth of substitution: an animal is substituted for a human victim, just as Temple sacrifice substitutes an animal for the original scapegoat murder. How is this story of (virtual) human sacrifice compatible with your gift theory?

Robert Daly: I agree with Girard that the story of the binding of Isaac (the *Akedah*) does indeed give us the key to the meaning of biblical sacrifice. Of course, we cannot hope to do justice to a story that has provoked voluminous commentary for several millennia. After all, early Christians frequently compared Jesus to Isaac, and many modern scholars see the Jewish oral interpretation of this story as central to Jesus's own understanding of his death. In the New Testament Epistles, Jesus is frequently compared to Isaac: Hebrews 11:17–19; Galatians 1:4 and 2:20; Ephesians 5:2, 25. In the rabbinic commentary on the *Akedah*, Isaac is portrayed as an adult who consents to his own binding (a reading consistent with Genesis). In short, what first appears as a story of coercive victimization becomes a kind of voluntary martyrdom—

René Girard (interrupting): Wait, if Isaac had volunteered, then why did Abraham have to bind him up?

Robert Daly: According to the rabbis, Isaac feared that he might lose his nerve at the last minute, so he asked his father to bind him. In this interpretation, despite God redeeming Isaac from death at the last minute, Isaac's action was a perfect sacrifice. The substitution of the ram is ignored. The true sacrifice is Isaac's self-sacrifice in giving himself wholly to God through obedience to his father. Christians, of course, adopted this rabbinic reading and applied it to Jesus's own self-sacrifice in perfect obedience to his father. Is the later Jewish and Christian understanding of self-sacrifice a mere metaphorical extension of the notion of sacrifice? On the contrary, self-sacrifice is the essential meaning of all sacrifice. Walter Burkert reminds us that many legends tell of animals that offered themselves up for sacrifice. Recall that all sacrifices are gifts. What is a gift? Philosophers have long argued that a gift is just a symbol of oneself: one's love, time, attention, and effort. Emerson memorably said that the ideal gift is a gift of the self—which explains why money usually makes a sorry gift. The offerings we present to God at the altar are but faint symbols of what we really owe him, namely, our very selves. Every sacrifice has meaning only insofar as it represents self-sacrifice. We give animals or cereal to God because we value them. Hence, the rabbis argued that all subsequent Temple sacrifices get their atoning power from the one perfect self-sacrifice of Isaac. Christians argue that Jesus's perfect self-sacrifice once and for all reconciles us to God.

John Milbank: René, until quite recently you rejected the whole notion that Jesus's death was some kind of self-sacrifice. For you, the whole notion of sacrifice embodies the appalling violence of what you call archaic religion. By revealing Jesus's death to be an unjust scapegoat murder, you claim that the Gospels seek to reveal the Satanic logic of the surrogate-victim mechanism and to free us from sacrifice forever. You acknowledge that the Gospel message was not generally received or understood among Christians, not even the earliest disciples. Hence, you wrote that "the Gospels never present the rule of the kingdom of God under the negative aspect of self-sacrifice"—knowing full well that the rest of the New Testament frequently refers to the death of Jesus as a sacrifice. In your animus against sacrifice you not only pit the New Testament against the Old (and the prophets against the priests), but you also pit the Gospels against the Epistles (Jesus against Paul). Is this a reasonable way to read the Bible?

René Girard: I have recanted my own rash "scapegoating" of sacrifice and of Hebrews. I was so horrified by the penal substitution theory of Jesus's death, in which an angry God demands the blood of his only Son as payment for the sins of mankind, that I rejected any sacrificial interpretation of the passion of Jesus. The penal substitution theory of atonement is a favorite among atheists who use it to discredit

Christianity. But I now realize that there are ways to interpret the death of Jesus as sacrificial without giving any quarter to archaic religion.

John Milbank: Your deep animus to the penal-substitution theory of Christian atonement, which I certainly share, is in some tension with your own theory of sacrifice as based on victim substitution. You have developed a penal-substitution theory of sacrifice but then recoil when it is applied to the sacrifice of Jesus. Some of your commentators claim that you have had a dramatic change of heart and mind regarding the meaning of sacrifice, but I think not. You continue to claim that Jesus's self-sacrifice has nothing in common with the burnt offerings of archaic religion. Instead of seeing a gradual development in how we give to God, from the offerings of valuable animals to Jesus's offering of his own life, you still see only an unbridgeable chasm between the irrational violence of animal sacrifice and the morally pure self-sacrifice of Jesus. You have now created two totally opposed meanings for the word "sacrifice": in Leviticus, "sacrifice" means murder, and in the Gospels, "sacrifice" means the refusal to murder. Allow me to quote you here (*Evolution and Conversion*): "No greater difference can be found: on the one hand, sacrifice as murder; on the other hand, sacrifice as the readiness to die in order not to participate in sacrifice as murder." This contrast would puzzle Jesus, who was known to instruct his followers to make their burnt offerings, as prescribed in Leviticus.

Joseph de Maistre: René, I am delighted, of course, that you have returned to the true Catholic faith of your childhood, but in your attacks on archaic religion you sound more like a Calvinist than a Catholic. Roman Christianity is marked above all by the dominance of priests, the "sacrifice" of the Mass, and many other practices shared with both ancient paganism and ancient Judaism. Calvin's reforms were directed precisely to abolish Catholic rituals, to extirpate the "sacrificial" interpretation of the Eucharist, and to purify Christianity from all vestiges of paganism. You call the Levitical priests—the ancient model of the Roman clergy—"murderers"! You always side with the Prophets in their scathing attacks on the priesthood and on empty rituals, especially the sacrificial rituals. Like Calvin, you see an unfathomable abyss separating ancient sacrifice from Christian ritual, and you frequently lament the return to all sorts of pagan practices: abortion, euthanasia, and sexual undifferentiation. Your critique of Levitical sacrifice looks like an attempt to purify Christianity of any remnants of Judaism.

The Catholic response to ancient Judaism and to ancient paganism is quite different. We acknowledge that due to the unity of the human race, there are no totally false religions. I have already pointed to the deep truths about sacrifice found in paganism and in Judaism. And John Henry Cardinal Newman argued that the fact that the Roman Church has adopted many rituals, offices, and institutions from paganism does not show that Romanism is nothing more than paganism—it simply shows that paganism is more than pagan. To paraphrase Newman, the fact that Christianity has adopted many of the offices, moral ideals, and rituals of Judaism does not show that Christianity is nothing more than Judaism—it just shows that Judaism is more than merely Jewish.

John Milbank: Girard's anthropology is not consistent with Reformed or with Catholic Christianity because it is not consistent with any religious dimension of human life. According to Girard, following Durkheim, all religious rituals function only to preserve and enhance human social unity. In this view, the highest good desired by human beings is social harmony; what people call "divine" is nothing more than the experience of that harmony. True, Girard and Durkheim acknowledge that human beings think of their rituals as attempts to communicate with transcendent beings, but they dismiss these subjective beliefs in favor of an objective account of how religion functions to promote social order. According to Girard, human beings are fully satisfied with social harmony, which they divinize in their religions. The only "god" is society itself.

But, according to Plato and Aristotle, not even to mention the Bible, human beings have a natural desire to understand their mortality and finitude in relation to divine beings who transcend time and space. Plato and Aristotle define human nature in terms of this quest for seeing the human drama in the context of the transcendent divine drama. So even though Plato and Aristotle are not remotely biblical or Christian in their theological beliefs, their anthropology is fully consistent with Christianity because it is open to the reality of the transcendent. Social harmony alone will never satisfy human beings, who by nature seek ultimate realities.

René Girard: I attack all ancient religions because their bloody rituals offer only the illusion of social harmony. They provide only ephemeral experiences of unity, which must be renewed daily with ever greater numbers of victims. Christianity alone, with its renunciation of violence, can provide a sound foundation for social harmony, peace, and right relation to our Creator. Yes, my scientific anthropology makes no reference to the human quest for the divine, because that quest is not subject to empirical confirmation. What we know about human beings from science is that we seek social unity and that we are willing to kill for it. Nonetheless, my anthropology provides a foundation for Christian theology because: first, I reveal the primordial violence of the human condition, what theologians call "original sin"; and second, I expose the utter failure of any purely human remedy for our violent condition. In this way, I limit my anthropology in order to make room for Christian faith.

Concluding Reflections on Violence

It is tempting to imagine a roundtable discussion on the topic of violence in which Girard is interrogated by other leading theorists of violence, such as Georges Sorel, Mahatma Gandhi, Frantz Fanon, and Hannah Arendt. Unfortunately, because these thinkers have such totally different conceptions of violence, they would simply talk past each other. For example, Sorel encourages the working class to use political and economic violence against the bourgeoisie. What does he mean by violence? Sorel's favorite example is a general strike. In other words, what Sorel means by violence is what Gandhi and Hannah Arendt mean by nonviolence. Similarly, whereas Fanon sees violence as empowering—"power grows out of the barrel of a gun," to use Mao's words—Arendt argues that violence usually reflects the absence of power. Thus, our theorists of violence are simply using the same word to talk about fundamentally different things. Such a conversation would quickly become very frustrating for all involved and would likely lead to violence—if only they could agree on what that is.

I will offer some reflections on Girard's theory of violence and raise some questions about it. In previous chapters, Girard's interlocutors have been quite blunt in their attacks on his theory; I will be much more tentative since in this chapter Girard is not here to defend himself. I will also offer some reflections on the usefulness of the whole notion of violence. Actual violence may be a big problem in the real world; the concept of "violence" is an even bigger problem in the world of ideas. Actual violence undermines progress in social and political life; the vagueness of the concept of "violence" undermines progress in the social sciences. In the vast literature that addresses the question of whether religion causes violence, there is a great deal of debate about the meaning and utility of the concept of "religion." Many writers find the whole notion of "religion" to be intolerably vague, yet virtually no one raises comparable questions about the idea of "violence." It is tempting but surely naïve to think that we might reduce real-world violence by reducing the vagueness of the concept of violence. Perhaps the whole notion of "violence" is the wrong way to think about the evils we deplore.

Every aspect of Girard's thought revolves around the concept of violence. Yet Girard never attempts to define violence; indeed, he even says that we cannot and should not attempt to define violence.[1] However, all of Girard's other framework concepts are defined in relation to violence, starting with desire: "Violence is the continuation of mimetic desire by violent means."[2] Desire is attracted to violence;[3] violence is always mingled with desire.[4] Desire is always rival-rous; and rivalry is always desirous. "Mimesis coupled with desire leads automatically to conflict."[5] Mimesis is the cause of the rivalry that leads to violence; violence is contagious through mimesis. A scapegoat is a victim of violence; sacrifice is the violent commemoration of the killing of the scapegoat. Girard sometimes even describes all violence in terms of sacri-fice: "If sacrifice resembles criminal violence, we may say that there is, inversely, hardly any form of violence that cannot be described in terms of sacrifice."[6] So whatever violence is, it involves desire, mimetic rivalry, scapegoating, and sacrifice.

Violence for Girard is like language for the French struc-turalists. We ordinarily think that we use language to further our purposes, but the structuralists argue that actually language is using us. How can language be an instrument when we cannot even think about our goals apart from language? Similarly, it is natural to think that we use violence as one of several possible means for accomplishing a purpose: shall I persuade this person to help me or simply coerce him? But for Girard, violence is not an instrument for achieving human purposes: violence has its own psycho-social logic quite apart from our individual purposes. We don't make use of violence; rather, violence makes use of us. Just as Clausewitz argued that war begins as the continuation of politics by other means and then escalates into mutual self-destruction, so Girardian violence follows a mimetic logic of vengeance and retaliation unrelated to our personal goals.[7] The real agent of social conflict is violence itself, which is why Girard often makes violence the grammatical subject of his social theory: "Violence is the divine force that everyone tries to use for his own purposes and that ends by using everyone for its own."[8] Violence is like Freudian libido, a hydraulic force that can be channeled but not repressed: "Violence too long held in check will overflow its bounds—and woe to those who happen to be nearby."[9]

Just as Simone Weil argues that violence—not Achilles or Hector—is the main protagonist of Homer's *Iliad*, so Girard argues that violence is the protagonist in the universal human drama.[10] There are other characters in the Girardian epic, and none of them are individual human beings. Desire, mimesis, and the surrogate-victim mechanism are all active protagonists with their own agendas. Desire does not belong to individuals; rather we are mere vehicles for desire;[11] similarly, we are caught up willy-nilly in the logic of mimetic rivalry and conflict. Finally, there is the surrogate-victim mechanism, who chooses victims and is both the hero and villain of the story.[12]

Girard never reconciled his scientific theory of violence with his personal abhorrence of it. Indeed, speaking as a scientist, he sometimes claims to have no moral agenda at all: "Contrary to what some think, I am not interested in defining what is good and bad in the social and cultural order."[13] Yet in other places, he speaks as a passionate moralist: "Violence is a terrible adversary, since it always wins. . . . We have to fight a violence that can no longer be controlled or mastered."[14] As a scientist, Girard claims that bad violence can be controlled only by good or sacred violence: "It must be admitted that, in order to prevent violence, we cannot do without a certain amount of violence." In this vein, he denies being a pacifist: "I should make it clear that I myself am not an unconditional pacifist, since I do not consider all forms of defense against violence to be illegitimate."[15] But as a passionate moralist and Christian, Girard frequently poses an apocalyptic dilemma: Either we renounce all violence or we face universal destruction. "The definitive renunciation of violence, without any second thoughts, will become for us the condition *sine qua non* for the survival of humanity itself and for each one of us."[16] He repeats this call to renounce violence in several different books and interviews.[17] Hence we face the irony that the intellectual leader of contemporary pacifism sometimes explicitly denies that he is a pacifist. Girard's inability to articulate a consistent moral response to violence reveals the unresolved tensions between his scientific functionalism and his personal moral passions.

Girard's theory of violence poses real challenges for those concerned with the ethical and political control of violence. If violence is not a matter of individual or political choice, then how can violence be subjected to ethical and political control?[18] If it is true, as Girard says, that "violence belongs to all men, and thus to none in particular," then how can we hold anyone in particular responsible for violence? Girard asks each person to renounce violence, but how can we renounce what does not belong to us?[19] Here we see the tension, again, between the two levels of this theory. As a theorist of social functioning, Girard says that "only violence can put an end to violence"[20] since ritual violence functions to restrain anarchic violence. Yet as a Christian peacemaker, Girard asks us to renounce all violence. Just as we saw with scapegoating and sacrifice, Girard's personal abhorrence of violence receives little support from his functionalism. Moreover, if we are to renounce violence, what does that mean? Girard never defines violence, but he does list various kinds of violence, including verbal violence, psychological violence, physical violence, and spiritual violence.[21] Since much of human conduct could be reasonably described as one of these kinds of violence, to renounce violence seems to require us to renounce most active human conduct entirely.

Girard sometimes distinguishes "good" from "bad" violence, not on the basis of moral criteria, but on the basis of social function. He argues that "beneficial violence must be carefully distinguished from harmful violence, and the former continually promoted at the expense of the latter. Ritual is nothing more than the regular exercise of 'good' violence."[22]

Bad violence, then, is the runaway conflict created by mimetic rivalry over scarce goods; it is a rivalry that soon escalates into a death feud and vendetta. "'Bad' violence," says Girard, "is by definition a force that works on various levels—physical, familial, social—and spreads from one to the other."[23] For individuals, this is the Hobbesian anarchy of the war of all against all; for states, this is the Clausewitzian descent into the absolute war of mutually-assured destruction. What makes "bad" violence bad? The fact that it destroys society, which is the highest possible value for a Durkheimian functionalism like Girard's. Just as viral diseases can only be countered by attenuated versions of the virus itself, so bad violence can only be countered by good violence: "violence can only be countered by more violence."[24] In other words, good violence inoculates us against potentially fatal outbursts of bad violence: "violence spreads through the group like a virus that only 'vaccination' by sacrifice can stop."[25]

What are examples of good violence? Society itself is built upon the foundation of selecting and then killing a scapegoat. Here all the bad violence between countless individuals is suspended and productively focused on a single victim, typically a marginal figure. Over time, this foundational lynching is routinized in the form of human and then animal sacrifice: "The function of sacrifice is to quell violence within the community and to prevent conflicts from erupting."[26] From sacrifices we move to the judicial exercise of good violence, first as trial by combat and then as legal punishment. Throughout this evolution, we see the same logic of all against one: in public prosecutions today, we describe the legal action as "the people vs. John Doe."[27] Girard explains that "just as the human body is a machine for transforming food into flesh and blood, generative unanimity is a process for changing bad violence into stability and fecundity."[28] The only difference that Girard sees between the violence of scapegoating and the violence of legal punishment is the degree of efficiency: "The judicial system and the institution of sacrifice share the same function, but the judicial system is infinitely more effective."[29]

Although we might insist that there is a fundamental distinction between killing an arbitrary victim—irrespective of guilt or innocence—and punishing someone determined by a court to be guilty, Girard often denies such a distinction. He says that the violence exercised by our modern penal system is not different from primitive revenge; he insists upon the "fundamental identity" of "vengeance, sacrifice, and legal punishment." He goes so far as to define legal punishment as "an institutionalized and legalized form of mob violence." All good violence, whether lynching or lawful punishment, is identical because it serves the same function of maintaining social harmony.[30] All distinctions between kinds of good violence fade to insignificance when compared to the apocalyptic dangers of bad violence: "A single careless gesture could unleash a holocaust in which society would be utterly destroyed."[31] If we are in permanent risk of an unlimited war of all against all, then distinctions between guilty and innocent victims appear to be mere legal niceties. Girard says that we must "give up the idea of retribution": it does not matter whether the victim is guilty or innocent. "What must be given up is the right to reprisals and even the right to what passes, in a number of cases, for legitimate defense."[32] Notice that Girard has implicitly elevated the value of social order above the value of justice. Perhaps killing one innocent scapegoat is worse than social anarchy? Isn't there an ancient Roman maxim, championed by Immanuel Kant: "let justice be done though the heavens fall"?

And although many of us make moral distinctions between justified and unjustified violence, between violence in self-defense and violence in aggression, Girard attacks these moral distinctions.[33] Let us begin with bad violence. In evaluating violence between individuals or between states, many people begin by attempting to distinguish a guilty aggressor from an innocent victim. But Girard believes that these common moral and legal distinctions ignore the true nature of violence, which is a cycle of mimetic blows and counter-blows that has no real beginning. Violence has its origin in the conflict generated by mimetic desire, not in any aggressive impulse. As we have seen, Girard denies that there is such a thing as aggression.[34] He believes that both parties to a violent conflict are equally guilty and equally innocent: "Physical violence is the perfect accomplishment of the conflictual mimetic relationship, and it is completely reciprocal. Everyone imitates the other's violence and returns it 'with interest'." Girard even terms the parties to a violent conflict "doubles" to underscore their essential identity and interchangeability.[35] In the cycle of reciprocal violence, there are no aggressors and no victims, no guilty and no innocent. He even says that killing and dying are identical: "To kill is to die, to die is to kill—for both stay within the circle of evil reciprocity, in which reprisals inevitably take place."[36] No party to a conflict considers himself the aggressor or the initiator of the conflict; each party interprets his own violence as purely defensive. Violence is a system of reciprocal actions that are beyond good or evil. Once we enter into the cycle of violence, we and our adversaries become what he calls "monstrous doubles."

As for good violence, that is, sacred violence, in choosing a victim for lynching or sacrifice, guilt or innocence is also irrelevant. Society simply needs to select an indifferent "sacrificiable victim" to absorb the sacred violence that would otherwise spread contagiously and become bad violence.[37] Neither the victim nor the crowd is guilty.[38] We know from experience, says Girard, that at least temporary social harmony will arise from lynching and from sacrifice quite independently of the objective guilt or innocence of the victim.

It is difficult to avoid the conclusion that Girard's theory of violence tells us more about our modern anxieties than about ancient religion. If true, this conclusion is ironic because it shows that the Girardian interpretation of ancient religion can be used to interpret Girard's own theory. Just as ancient man projected his social anxieties onto his religious rituals, so Girard projects modern social anxieties onto ancient religion. As we have seen, Girard argues that ancient religious rituals, which seem to be about harmony with God, are actually about social harmony. Instead of worshipping God, says Girard, ancient religions are actually worshipping the power of society. For example, when ancient priests offered sacrifices to the gods, they were actually commemorating the foundation of their society. Durkheim's students, Hubert and Mauss, pioneered this sociological interpretation of ancient sacrifice:

"The sacred things in relation to which sacrifice functions, are social things. . . . It is a social function because sacrifice is concerned with social matters."[39] Again, sacrifice is not about the gods, it is about social harmony. In his own sociological interpretation of sacrifice, Girard is following the Durkheimians very closely.

Some scholars today argue that the Durkheimian theory of religion is itself largely a projection of contemporary social anxieties upon ancient religious myths and rituals. Durkheim's theory of religion turned out to be itself Durkheimian. Ivan Strenski persuasively shows that Durkheim and his French disciples made the theory of sacrifice central to their account of religion because of long-standing debates in French society about the moral significance of the sacrifice of individuals to the state, especially in relation to the Dreyfus affair and the First World War. The pressing issue of their own society was whether citizens had a duty to sacrifice their own lives for the good of France. Because civic sacrifice was so salient in the France of their day, the Durkheimians made ritual sacrifice the centerpiece of ancient religion. As Strenski says: "For although it seems obvious that Hubert and Mauss's [book] *Sacrifice* is about *ritual* sacrifice, the book ends with a passionate discourse on *civic* duty!" For this reason, Strenski is right to ask about Girard: "How much of what he says about ritual sacrifice projects his own *moralist* and pacifist politics?"[40] After the unprecedented killing during the first half of the twentieth century, anxiety about human violence has been pervasive. In the wake of the modern Holocaust, ancient holocausts were bound to be seen in a new and sinister light. Indeed, the year 1972 saw the simultaneous publications of Girard's *Violence and the Sacred* and Walter Burkert's equally dark interpretation of ritual sacrifice, *Homo Necans*.[41] Clearly, the crisis of modern political violence has deeply shaped these interpretations of ancient religion.[42]

Whatever its merits as an explanation of ancient religion, Girard's functional analysis of violence has a bracing moral realism. He acknowledges the deep and tenacious hold that rivalry, hatred, and revenge have on human life. This tenacity explains why only something as coercive as violence itself could possibly restrain the dangers of anarchic violence. Like Hobbes, Girard implicitly argues that in the game of society, clubs are trumps. This explains why we allow public authorities to use violence in ways that would otherwise be condemned as kidnapping, battery, or murder. We acknowledge the need to counter violence with more violence, as Girard says. So it is deeply puzzling why Girard then insists upon heaping abuse on preventive and curative violence by condemning scapegoating, sacrifice, and criminal justice. He frequently denounces priests and scapegoaters as murderers and persecutors, yet he never denounces those who participate in mimetic rivalry and contagious violence. In short, he denounces only the practitioners of good violence. I wish Girard had explained more fully how violence can be functionally good but morally bad. His scientific functionalism is never fully harmonized with his moral convictions.

Girard's Christianity is also never truly reconciled with his functionalism. On the one hand, Girard acknowledges that functionally, Christianity is a disaster: by undermining the beliefs that supported scapegoating and sacrifice, Christianity weakens the effectiveness of sacred violence to control anarchic violence. Christianity, then, he says, leaves us with an apocalyptic choice between a renouncement of all violence and a global conflagration of (nuclear) violence. In this mood, he never explains why legal justice cannot serve as the functional equivalent of sacred violence. On the other hand, he also presents Christianity as offering a functional solution to the eternal challenge of human violence. Christianity, he says, teaches us to renounce violence. But according to Girard, mimetic rivalry and conflict operate below the level of our conscious beliefs. It follows then that no mere conscious renunciation of violence could possibly immunize us from contagious violence. Here Girard points to the mimetic function of Christianity: the only way to defeat mimetic rivalry is to imitate Christ. Only Christian mimesis can disarm the power of mimetic conflict. However, before we can imitate Christ we must have a desire to imitate him, and as we have seen, Girard has no account of how we form our tutelary desires. Thus, within his account of mimetic desire, Girard cannot explain or justify the desire to imitate Christ. Neither the apocalyptic dilemma he poses nor the Christian mimesis he favors finds adequate support in his scientific theory of desire, mimesis, and violence.

Yet perhaps the shortcomings of Girard's theory of violence stem from the fundamental indeterminacy of the very idea of "violence." We should not expect more precision in a science than its subject matter will bear. Perhaps the whole notion of "violence" is the wrong starting point for thinking about coercion, cruelty, harm, and killing. If we extend the notion of violence beyond the physical, as Girard does, to include verbal, psychological, and spiritual violence, then we have included virtually every human deed. After all, anything I do or say might be described by someone as verbal, psychological, or spiritual violence. To say anything meaningful is to offend someone. Therefore, renouncing violence in this broad sense would mean renouncing an active human life. Here pacifism really is pure quietism.

What if we limit the notion of violence to the realm of the physical? The first definition of violence in the *Oxford English Dictionary* is: "The exercise of physical force so as to inflict injury on, or cause damage to, persons or property." By this definition, a hurricane is violent, an accident is violent, and demolition is violent. Similarly, by this definition a non-violent world literally means a world without natural disasters, without accidents, without punishment, and without demolition. In short, the notion of violence here focuses our attention on only the most superficial, visible, and physical aspects of a situation. But the evil we deplore is not physical at all, even if it can have physical effects.

The violent, like the miraculous, is always dramatic. What makes violence and miracle dramatic is that both disrupt the normal course of events. If the natural unfolding of events forms our background expectations, then violence and the miraculous both appear contrary to nature. Moreover, violence and miracle both appear as dramatic and external alterations of the natural unfolding of things. This is why violence is associated with force—only force can alter the normal course of things. What makes the violent and the miraculous different? Only that one is dreaded, while the other is welcomed.

At the foundation of the notion of violence is the emotional arousal we feel in the face of sudden and usually unexpected changes to things we care about. We usually think of these dramatic changes in terms of harm or destruction because sudden and unexpected change is usually for the worse. If healing were as sudden and unexpected as injury or if growth were as sudden and unexpected as death can be, then healing and growth would also be full of dramatic arousal for us. If a building could rise up as quickly as it can fall, building would be as dramatic as destroying. We associate hatred with violence because hatred often causes sudden and unexpected change in the world, such as assault and murder. When love causes sudden and unexpected change in the world, we call that miraculous.

There is a puzzling asymmetry in human life: sudden, dramatic, and visible change is usually injurious or destructive, while growth, education, moral uplift, and spiritual progress are gradual and largely invisible. Perhaps movement toward lower levels of entropy always takes more time than movement toward higher levels. Put differently, in the drama of human life, violence is much more common than miracle. It is delightful though perhaps useless to imagine a miraculous world in which growth were as sudden as death, in which love were instantly life-altering, and in which moral conversion were as dramatic as a shooting. Perhaps giving birth is the best example of a sudden and sometimes unexpected change for the good—and giving birth does seem in some ways both violent and miraculous.

Clearly, we are emotionally aroused by sudden and unexpected change in things we care about. Given that such change is usually for the worse, our arousal is unsurprising. Our survival often depends upon an appropriate response to such dramatic events. Producers of rhetoric and visual media frequently exploit these emotional triggers—hence, the motto of the newsroom: "If it bleeds, it leads." What gets our attention is not gradual healing, slow moral uplift, or the transformative power of love over time, but sudden and unexpected changes in things important to us—which usually involve lots of blood. Hence, we are more likely to be traumatized by bloody but superficial wounds than by a diagnosis of dementia. There is no doubt that violence is emotionally salient, which means that violence will always be a fundamental concept in politics, for what is emotionally salient to many people is also thereby politically salient. In politics, violence is significant whether it be due to natural disaster, plague, accident, or malice. Politicians must manage violence no matter what its cause.

But in the ethical deliberations of individuals, whether they be political leaders or ordinary citizens, the notion of violence is too vague and too superficial to be helpful. Violence refers only to the visible and physical aspects of a situation, while moral actions are defined by the invisible intentions of agents. Thus, though the physical violence of a battlefield amputation or a car accident might be identical to a murderous assault, they are utterly different kinds of deeds. Shooting someone in self-defense might be visibly indistinguishable from murdering someone, but the moral significance of the two deeds could not be more opposed. As moral agents deliberating about damage, injury, or death, we should not focus on blood, force, or violence. Instead, we should focus on the motives and intentions of agents: were they being vicious, cruel, or indifferent, or were they being just, caring, or responsible? What makes violent acts morally wrong—when they are in fact morally wrong—is not that they are violent: after all, surgery and accidents are not morally wrong, yet they are violent. A surgeon and a torturer might use the same instruments and cause the same injuries, but surgery is not torture. Instead of renouncing violence, we ought to instead renounce cruelty, hatred, indifference, fanaticism, sadism, and arrogance. We must also recognize that love sometimes requires us to punish, to coerce, and to perform surgery—there is such a thing as "tough love." If evil were a function of physical force rather than of spiritual hatred, we would be compelled to say that General Omar Bradley, who used physical violence to defeat Hitler, was morally worse than Joseph Goebbels, who used non-violent but hateful speech to support Hitler.[43]

Why is the language of violence so common in discussions of human evil? I think it is because the concept of violence draws our attention to the most emotionally salient aspects of human suffering: force, destruction, blood, and dismemberment. We have a powerful instinctive attraction and repulsion to violence, just as we do to pornography: sex and violence dominate our imagination. But we must not confuse emotional salience with moral salience. A violent act of hatred is not necessarily worse than a non-violent one. Is spanking worse than verbally humiliating a child? Is slapping in private worse than slandering in public? Is the guillotine morally worse than lethal injection? Violent evils are more dramatic but not inherently morally worse than non-violent evils. Indeed, by focusing on violence we can easily lose sight of the moral questions raised by painless and bloodless killing, whether performed as capital punishment or as euthanasia. Violence is simply not a useful concept for ethical deliberation about human action.

What lessons does Girard's theory have for the practical reasoning of morally good persons? I think his ideas provide a useful set of cautionary tales, all of which chasten our pride. First, Girard reminds us that although we love to think of ourselves as unique, in many of our passions and ideals we are just like everyone else. What this means is that we are vulnerable to social contagions. Social contagions are real, though not always serious. For instance, when we think we are choosing a unique name for our special baby, we are usually choosing the same name as everyone else in our society at that moment. But other social contagions lead to murderous hatreds. Second, Girard reminds us that we should interrogate our social practices of exclusion. Who are the scapegoats in our society: homosexuals, transsexuals, the unborn, the mentally ill, or the obese? In our small acts of exclusion we unknowingly pave the way for deadly acts of exclusion. Third, our encounter with Girard should lead us to interrogate our competitive urges and rivalries: what do we lose by winning? Rivalries easily generate conflict, and Girard shows us how easy it is for conflicts to escalate into mutual destruction. Finally, though we are all tempted to think of ourselves as being fully sovereign over our own desires, goals, and conduct, Girard shows us that we are at best only partly sovereign over our very selves.[44] These are all invaluable lessons in humility.

We can now say with some confidence that Girard's most important intellectual and cultural legacy has been to provide a worldview for pacifism. If Darwin can be said to have made atheism intellectually respectable, then Girard has done the same for pacifism. Before Girard, pacifists had little more than the sayings of Jesus, supplemented by St. Francis, Tolstoy, Gandhi, and the Dalai Lama. Because of Girard, pacifists now possess a psychology, sociology, anthropology, and theology of peacemaking. There are many ironies here. Girard's views that human nature is essentially prone to violence, that violence is often needed to control violence, and, of course, that religion itself stems from violence, do not seem promising, at first, as grounds for pacifism. Should peacemakers look to Girard to diagnose and to remedy the violence all around us? That is the chief question I have sought to illuminate in this book.

Notes

1 "What does violence mean objectively? I don't think we can define it. I don't even think we should try." René Girard, "Mimesis, Sacrifice, and the Bible," in *Sacrifice, Scripture, and Substitution*, ed. Ann W. Astell and Sandor Goodhart (Notre Dame, IN: University of Notre Dame Press, 2011), 65–66. Cf. Girard, "Interview," in *Mimesis and Science*, ed. Scott R. Garrels (East Lansing: Michigan State University Press, 2011), 215–252, at 248.

2 René Girard, "Discussion," in *Violent Origins*, ed. Robert G. Hamerton-Kelly (Stanford: Stanford University Press, 1987), 106–145, at 123.

3 René Girard, *Violence and the Sacred*, trans. Patrick Gregory (Baltimore: Johns Hopkins University Press, 1977), 151.

4 Girard, *Violence and the Sacred*, 145.

5 Girard, *Violence and the Sacred*, 146.

6 Girard, *Violence and the Sacred*, 1.

7 See René Girard and Benoît Chantre: *Battling to the End*, trans. Mary Baker (East Lansing: Michigan State University Press, 2010). The title of the French original is *Achever Clausewitz*. For a

more "dialectical" reading of Clausewitz, see Richard Ned Lebow, *The Tragic Vision of Politics* (Cambridge: Cambridge University Press, 2003), chap. 5.

8 Girard, *Violence and the Sacred*, 144.

9 Girard, *Violence and the Sacred*, 30; "When unappeased, violence seeks and always finds a surrogate victim" (2).

10 "For violence so crushes whomever it touches that it appears at last external no less to him who dispenses it than to him who endures it." Simone Weil, "The *Iliad*, Poem of Might," in *The Simone Weil Reader*, ed. George A. Panichas (New York: David McKay, 1977), 153–183, at 167. Girard expresses his debt to Simone Weil in *Evolution and Conversion: Dialogues on the Origins of Culture*, René Girard with Pierpaolo Antonello and João Cezar de Castro Rocha (London: T.J. Clark, 2007), 150, and "Conversation with René Girard," by Phil Rose in *Contagion* 18 (2011): 23–38, at 26.

11 "Desire is responsible for its own evolution." René Girard, *Things Hidden Since the Foundation of the World*, trans. Stephen Bann and Michael Metteer (Stanford: Stanford University Press, 1987), 304.

12 "The victim of mimetic snowballing is chosen by the contagion itself." René Girard, *I See Satan Fall Like Lightning*, trans. James G. Williams (New York: Orbis, 2001), 24. He speaks of "a scape-goat chosen by mimeticism itself" in *Sacrifice*, trans. Matthew Pattillo and David Dawson (East Lansing: Michigan State University Press, 2001), 26.

13 René Girard, *The Scapegoat*, trans. Yvonne Freccero (Baltimore: Johns Hopkins University Press, 1986), 19.

14 René Girard, "On War and Apocalypse," *First Things*, Aug/Sept 2009, http://www.firstthings.com/article/2009/08/apocalypse-now.

15 René Girard, *The One by Whom Scandal Comes*, trans. Malcolm B. DeBevoise (East Lansing: Michigan State University Press, 2014), 98 and 131.

16 Girard, *Things Hidden Since the Foundation of the World*, 137.

17 "Violence must be renounced, unilaterally if need be, or universal destruction will ensue." He says of Christian pacifism: "It is the scientific *sine qua non* of bare survival." René Girard, *To Double Business Bound* (Baltimore: Johns Hopkins University Press, 1978), 227. "We can all participate in the divinity of Christ so long as we renounce our own violence." Girard, "On War and Apocalypse," http://www.firstthings.com/article/2009/08/apocalypse-now. "Sooner or later, either humanity will

renounce violence . . . or it will destroy the planet." Girard, *Battling to the End*, 21.

18 "The unanimous mimeticism of the scapegoat is the true ruler of human society." Girard, *The Scapegoat*, 145.

19 Girard, *Violence and the Sacred*, 257, and *Things Hidden*, 137.

20 Girard, *Violence and the Sacred*, 26.

21 See Girard, "Generative Scapegoating," in *Violent Origins*, 79, and *Violence and the Sacred*, 151 and 153.

22 Girard, *Violence and the Sacred*, 37. Although Girard often puts the expressions "bad" violence and "good" violence in scare quotes, he also earnestly distinguishes beneficial from harmful violence.

23 Girard, *Violence and the Sacred*, 58.

24 Girard, *Violence and the Sacred*, 31. For Girard's view that bad violence is like disease and good violence is like a vaccine, see pp. 32 and 290. Girard even claims that vaccination was invented on the model of the preventive function of sacrifice: "Now we can see that vaccination, like so many other human institutions, really amounts to a metaphorical displacement of sacrifice." *Violence and the Sacred*, 290.

25 Girard, *Battling to the End*, 23.

26 Girard, *Violence and the Sacred*, 14. "The sacrificial process prevents the spread of violence by keeping vengeance in check" (18).

27 Speaking of legal punishment, Girard says: "The concept can be traced back to spontaneous unanimity, to the irresistible conviction that compels an entire community to vent its fury on a single individual." *Violence and the Sacred*, 299.

28 Girard, *Violence and the Sacred*, 266.

29 Girard, *Violence and the Sacred*, 23.

30 Girard, *Violence and the Sacred*, 16, 25, and 299. Elsewhere he adds: "capital punishment is already ritual murder." *Evolution and Conversion*, 73.

31 Girard, *Violence and the Sacred*, 283.

32 Girard, *Things Hidden*, 198.

33 Speaking of the "refusal to allow any distinctions . . . between legitimate and illegitimate violence," Girard says: "This refusal is in itself quite reasonable and commendable." *Things Hidden*, 399.

34 Girard: "Aggression does not exist." *Battling to the End*, 18.

35 Girard, *Things Hidden*, 300 and 302.

36 Girard, *Things Hidden*, 214.

37 Girard, *Violence and the Sacred*, 4.

38 "No one is really guilty. The victims cannot be condemned for

exerting their evil influence. . . . But the violence that directly or indirectly emanated from the community cannot be condemned, either: there was no other course." Girard, "Generative Scapegoating," 96.

39 Henri Hubert and Marcel Mauss, *Sacrifice: Its Nature and Function*, trans. W. D. Halls (Chicago: University of Chicago Press, 1964), 101–102.

40 Ivan Strenski, "The Social and Intellectual Origins of Hubert and Mauss's Theory of Ritual Sacrifice," in *India and Beyond: Aspects of Literature, Meaning, Ritual and Thought*, ed. Dick van der Meij (London: Kegan Paul, 1997), 511–537, at 512. Emphasis his.

41 See Walter Burkert, *Homo Necans: The Anthropology of Ancient Greek Sacrificial Ritual and Myth*, trans. Peter Bing (Berkeley: University of California Press, 1983). In his preface to the English translation, Burkert refers to "René Girard's *Violence and the Sacred*, which appeared in the same year as *Homo Necans* and may be seen as largely parallel in intent." (xiii).

42 Speaking of Burkert and Girard, Mary Douglas says: "Their writings, which in our time have colored so heavily the interpretation of ancient religion, are themselves colored by their own period. First, the guilt of the Holocaust, and then revulsion against violence and cruelty during the Vietnam War and after." See her "Go-Away Goat," in *The Book of Leviticus*, ed. Rolf Rendtorff and Robert A. Kugler (Leiden: Brill, 2003), 121–141, at 124.

43 Reinhold Niebuhr used this contrast to criticize pacifists.

44 "Mimetic theory, in this sense, has a strong ethical component; for it acknowledges that we are all oriented towards a violence that is mimetically engendered." Girard, *Evolution and Conversion*, 172.

Guide to Further Reading

Preface: Why Girard? Why Dialogue?

With the recent rise of militant Islam, there has been an explosion of interest in the idea that religion gives rise to violence. For a survey of this debate, see Mark Juergensmeyer and Margo Kitts (editors), *Princeton Readings in Religion and Violence* (Princeton: Princeton University Press, 2011). Girard is best known for the converse claim, namely that violence gave rise to religious rituals—a view that stems from late nineteenth-century anthropology. A pioneering study is William Robertson Smith, *Lectures on the Religion of the Semites* (London: A. & C. Black, 1927, and Sheffield: Sheffield Academic Press, 1995). For a contemporary assessment of Smith, see Bernhard Maier, *William Robertson Smith: His Life, His Work, and His Times* (Tübingen: Mohr Siebeck, 2009). Another Victorian pioneer of religious anthropology is Gilbert Murray, whose classic book is *Five Stages of Greek Religion* (Boston: Beacon, 1951). On Murray's work in the context of his colleagues at Cambridge, see *The Cambridge Ritualists: An Annotated Bibliography of the Works by and about Jane Ellen Harrison, Gilbert Murray, Francis M. Cornford, and Arthur Bernard Cook*, by Shelley Arlen (Metuchen, NJ: Scarecrow Press, 1990). The Cambridge Ritualists argued that myths are based on religious rituals, the basis of Girard's view that myths are rooted in scapegoat and sacrificial rituals. In his classic book *Totem and Taboo* (New York: W. W. Norton, 1989), Sigmund Freud also argued that violence gave rise to religious rituals—a book that directly inspired Girard's book, *Violence and the Sacred*, translated by Patrick Gregory (Baltimore: Johns Hopkins University Press, 1977).

Girard is the last of the grand theorists of the human sciences. For other examples of such comprehensive theories, see *Karl Marx: A Reader*, edited by Jon Elster (Cambridge: Cambridge University Press, 1986); *The Basic Writings of Sigmund Freud*, edited A. A. Brill (New York: Modern Library, 1995); *Max Weber: Selections in Translation*, edited by W. G. Runciman and translated by Eric Matthews (Cambridge: Cambridge University Press, 1978); and *Readings from Emile Durkheim*, edited by Kenneth Thompson (London: Routledge, 2004).

For some excellent expositions of Girard's thought, I recommend Chris Fleming, *René Girard: Violence and Mimesis* (Cambridge: Polity, 2004); Michael Kirwan, *Discovering Girard* (Cambridge, MA: Cowley, 2005); and Wolfgang Palaver, *René Girard's Mimetic Theory*, translated by Gabriel Borrud (East Lansing: Michigan State University Press, 2013). Gil Bailie's book *Violence Unveiled: Humanity at the Crossroads* (New York: Crossroad, 1995) both explains and develops Girard's thought in new directions.

Chapter Two: Why Do We Read Literature? A Symposium
Girard's theory of the scientific value of great literature is found in all of his books, but see especially *Deceit, Desire and the Novel: Self and Other in Literary Structure*, translated by Yvonne Freccero (Baltimore: Johns Hopkins University Press, 1966); *To Double Business Bound: Essays on Literature, Mimesis, and Anthropology* (Baltimore: Johns Hopkins University Press, 1978); *A Theater of Envy: William Shakespeare* (New York: Oxford University Press, 1991); *Oedipus Unbound: Selected Writings on Rivalry and Desire*, edited by Mark R. Anspach (Stanford: Stanford University Press, 2004); and *Mimesis and Theory: Essays on Literature and Criticism, 1953–2005*, edited by Robert Doran (Stanford: Stanford University Press, 2008). Girard's stark contrast between myth and Gospel is found in *Things Hidden Since the Foundation of the World*, translated by Stephen Bann and Michael Metteer (Stanford: Stanford University Press, 1987). For a study of Girard's reading of myths, see Richard Joseph Golsan, *René Girard and Myth: An Introduction* (New York: Garland, 1993).

A fine introduction to debates in the philosophy of literature is Eileen John and Dominic McIver Lopes, editors, *Philosophy of Literature: Contemporary and Classic Readings* (Malden, MA: Blackwell Publishers, 2004). For Cole Porter's theory of literature as a mating song, see *Cole Porter: Selected Lyrics*, edited by Roger Kimball (New York: Library of America, 2006). Oscar Wilde argues for the supremacy of beauty over morality in all of his dramas, but see his *The Critic as Artist* (London: James R. Osgood McIlvaine, 1891). Simone Weil's classic essays on beauty and art in relation to God are found in *The Simone Weil Reader*, edited by George A. Panichas (Ann Arbor: University of Michigan Press, 1977).

Socrates's theory of art is found in Plato's dialogues *Ion* and *Republic* in *Plato: The Complete Works*, edited by John M. Cooper and D. S. Hutchinson (Indianapolis, IN: Hackett Publishing, 1997). Aristotle's theory of art (*technē*) is found in his *Physics* and his *Metaphysics*; his theory of imitation in narratives is found in his

Poetics. See *The Complete Works of Aristotle,* edited by Jonathan Barnes (Princeton: Princeton University Press, 1984).

Immanuel Kant's theory of art and of the sublime is found in *The Critique of Judgement,* translated by James Creed Meredith (New York: Oxford University Press, 2007). Kant emphasizes the complex relation of art to practical reason, a theme developed by Lisa Zunshine in *Why We Read Fiction: Theory of Mind and the Novel* (Columbus: Ohio State University Press, 2006) and by Paisley Livingston in *Literature and Rationality: Ideas of Agency in Theory and Fiction* (Cambridge: Cambridge University Press, 1991). Jerome Stolnitz rejects these claims in his essay "On the Cognitive Triviality of Art" in John and Lopes (editors), *Philosophy of Literature.* The theory of the sublime was pioneered by Cassius Longinus (AD 213–273); see his *Longinus on the Sublime,* translated by A. O. Prickard (Oxford: Clarendon Press, 1930). Kant's "analytic of the sublime" develops the thought of Edmund Burke's *A Philosophical Enquiry into the Origin of Our Ideas of the Sublime and Beautiful,* edited by Adam Phillips (Oxford: Oxford University Press, 1990).

Leo Tolstoy's moralizing theory of art is found in his *What is Art?,* translated by Richard Pevear and Larissa Volokhonsky (New York: Penguin, 1995). Wayne Booth also develops a moral theory of literature in *The Company We Keep: An Ethics of Fiction* (Berkeley: University of California Press, 1989). Similarly, Martha Nussbaum sees literature as serving to refine our moral perceptions in *Love's Knowledge: Essays on Philosophy and Literature* (New York: Oxford University Press, 1990). C. S. Lewis discusses the relationship of literature to evil in his *Preface to Paradise Lost* (London: Oxford University Press, 1961).

Sigmund Freud developed his theory of art as play in "Creative Writers and Day-Dreaming" in John and Lopes (editors), *Philosophy of Literature.* Freud's theory of art as play has been developed by Kendall L. Walton in his *Mimesis as Make-Believe: On the Foundations of the Representational Arts* (Cambridge, MA: Harvard University Press, 1990). On the role of play in human culture more generally, see Johan Huizinga, *Homo Ludens: A Study of the Play-Element in Culture* (Boston: Beacon Press, 1955).

Chapter Three: Mimetic Desire: A Conversation with William James

Girard's theory of mimetic desire was first formulated in his book *Deceit, Desire and the Novel.* He has developed his account of mimetic desire in *Mimesis and Theory* (2008); *When These Things Begin:*

Conversations with Michel Treguer, translated by Trevor Cribben Merrill (East Lansing: Michigan State University Press, 2014); and *Anorexia and Mimetic Desire,* translated by Mark R. Anspach (East Lansing: Michigan State University Press, 2013). Girard's engagement with the thought of Carl von Clausewitz (1780–1831) led to a new emphasis on mimetic desire leading to mutual destruction. See Girard's *Battling to the End: Conversations with Benoît Chantre,* translated by Mary Baker (East Lansing: Michigan State University Press, 2010). For Clausewitz's classic work on the logic of war, see his *On War,* edited and translated by Michael Howard and Peter Paret (Princeton: Princeton University Press, 1984). For an important philosophical critique of Girard's theory of mimetic desire, see Paisley Livingston, *Models of Desire: René Girard and the Psychology of Mimesis* (Baltimore: Johns Hopkins University Press, 1992).

On Aristotle's theory of desire, see his *On the Soul* in *The Complete Works of Aristotle,* edited by Jonathan Barnes. On Kant's theory of human social rivalry, what he calls "asocial sociality," see his "Idea of a Universal History on a Cosmopolitan Plan" (1784).

On Freud's theory of desire (*libido*), see *The Basic Writings of Sigmund Freud,* edited by A. A. Brill. For Kurt Lewin's "field theory" of desire, see his "The Conflict Between Aristotelian and Galileian Modes of Thought in Contemporary Psychology," *Journal of General Psychology* 5 (1931).

On Edward L. Thorndike's research on imitation in animal learning, see his *Reward and Punishment in Animal Learning* (Baltimore: Johns Hopkins University Press, 1932).

William James's theory of desire, habit, and imitation can be found in his classic *Principles of Psychology* (Cambridge, MA: Harvard University Press, 1981). James's study in the psychology of religion is *The Varieties of Religious Experience* (Cambridge, MA: Harvard University Press, 1984). James's theories of war, violence, and pacifism can be found in his essay "The Moral Equivalent of War" in his *Essays on Faith and Morals* (New York: Longmans, Green, and Co., 1943).

Girard's theory of mimesis has its origins in Gabriel Tarde's classic *The Laws of Imitation,* translated by Elsie Worthington Clews Parsons (New York: Henry Holt, 1903). For studies of the scientific basis of Girard's mimetic theory, see *Mimesis and Science: Empirical Research on Imitation and the Mimetic Theory of Culture and Religion,* edited by Scott R. Garrels (East Lansing: Michigan State University Press, 2011); Paul Dumouchel, editor, *Violence and Truth: On the Work of René Girard* (Stanford: Stanford University Press, 1988); and Jean-Michel Oughourlian, *The Genesis of Desire,* translated by Eugene

Webb (East Lansing: Michigan State University Press, 2010). For further studies on the psychology of imitation, see John A. Bargh and Tanya L. Chartrand, "The Unbearable Automaticity of Being," *American Psychologist* 54/7 (1999): 462–479; Susan Hurley and Nick Chater, *Perspectives on Imitation: From Neuroscience to Social Science* (Cambridge, MA: M.I.T. Press, 2005); and Jennifer Radden, *On Delusion* (London: Routledge, 2011).

Chapter Four: A Crowd of Theories

Girard's theory of crowds is found in all of his books, but see especially: *Violence and the Sacred*; *The Scapegoat*, translated by Yvonne Freccero (Baltimore: Johns Hopkins University Press, 1986); "Generative Scapegoating" in *Violent Origins*, edited by Robert G. Hamerton-Kelly (Stanford: Stanford University Press, 1987); "Peter's Denial and the Question of Mimesis" in *Notre Dame English Journal* 14/3 (1982): 177–189; and *The One by Whom Scandal Comes*, translated by Malcolm B. DeBevoise (East Lansing: Michigan State University Press, 2014).

For Elias Canetti's highly original take on crowds, see his *Crowds and Power*, translated by Carol Stewart (New York: Seabury, 1978). Freud's theory of crowd psychology is found in *Mass Psychology and Other Writings*, translated by J. A. Underwood and Jacqueline Rose (London: Penguin, 2004).

On the theory of the "crowd mind" see Gustave Le Bon, *The Crowd: A Study of the Popular Mind* (London: T. Fisher Unwin, 1914); Emile Durkheim, *The Elementary Forms of Religious Life*, translated by Karen E. Fields (New York: Free Press, 1955); Paul Guillaume, *Imitation in Children*, translated by Elaine P. Halperin (Chicago: University of Chicago Press, 1971); and William McDougall, *The Group Mind, a Sketch of the Principles of Collective Psychology, with Some Attempt to Apply Them to the Interpretation of National Life and Character* (New York: G.P. Putnam's Sons, 1920).

For critiques of the psychology of the "crowd mind" see Floyd Henry Allport, *The Group Fallacy in Relation to Social Science* (Hanover, NH: Sociological Press, 1927) and Gordon Allport, *ABC's of Scapegoating* (New York: Anti-Defamation League of B'nai B'rith, 1969).

For the view that modern sociology emerged from the politics of crowds, see Christian Borch, *The Politics of Crowds: An Alternative History of Sociology* (Cambridge: Cambridge University Press, 2012). On the sociology, psychology, and politics of crowds, see J. S. McClelland, *The Crowd and the Mob: From Plato to Canetti* (London:

Unwin Hyman, 1989); Serge Moscovici, *The Age of the Crowd: A Historical Treatise on Mass Psychology*, translated by J. C. Whitehouse (Cambridge: Cambridge University Press, 1985); and James Surowiecki, *The Wisdom of Crowds* (New York: Doubleday, 2004). For an analysis of the logical structure of all possible crowds, see Sam Wright, *Crowds and Riots: A Study in Social Organization* (Beverly Hills, CA: Sage Publications, 1978).

Chapter Five: Scapegoating Sacrifice: A Discussion Moderated by John Milbank

Girard's theory of sacrifice in relation to the Bible can be found in several of his books, including *Things Hidden Since the Foundation of the World*, translated by Stephen Bann and Michael Metteer (Stanford: Stanford University Press, 1987); *I See Satan Fall Like Lightning*, translated by James G. Williams (New York: Orbis Books, 2001); *Sacrifice*, translated by Matthew Pattillo and David Dawson (East Lansing: Michigan State University Press, 2011); and (with) Gianni Vattimo, *Christianity, Truth, and Weakening Faith: A Dialogue*, edited by Pierpaolo Antonello and translated by William MacCuaig (New York: Columbia University Press, 2010). See also, Rebecca Adams, "Violence, Difference, Sacrifice: A Conversation with René Girard," *Religion and Literature* 25/2 (1993): 9–33.

For the intellectual background of Girard's theory of sacrifice, see Owen Bradley, *A Modern Maistre: The Social and Political Thought of Joseph de Maistre* (Lincoln: University of Nebraska Press, 1999); Henri Hubert and Marcel Mauss, *Sacrifice: Its Nature and Function*, translated by W. D. Halls (Chicago: University of Chicago Press, 1964); and Ivan Strenski, *Contesting Sacrifice: Religion, Nationalism, and Social Thought in France* (Chicago: University of Chicago Press, 2002), *Theology and the First Theory of Sacrifice* (Leiden: Brill, 2003), and "The Social and Intellectual Origins of Hubert and Mauss's Theory of Ritual Sacrifice," in *India and Beyond: Aspects of Literature, Meaning, Ritual and Thought*, edited by Dick Van Der Meij (London: Kegan Paul, 1997): 511–537.

John Milbank places Girard's theory of sacrifice in the context of many other theories in "Stories of Sacrifice: From Wellhausen to Girard," in *Theory, Culture, and Society* 12/4 (1995): 15–46. Joseph de Maistre's dark meditations on sacrifice can be found in *Saint Petersburg Dialogues*, translated by Richard Lebrun (Montreal: McGill-Queen's University Press, 1993). Jacob Milgrom's theory of biblical sacrifice is found in his commentary: *The Anchor Bible: Leviticus 1–16* (New York: Doubleday, 1991). Robert Daly's theory of

Christian sacrifice is found in *The Origins of the Christian Doctrine of Sacrifice* (Philadelphia: Fortress Press, 1977) and *Christian Sacrifice: The Judeo-Christian Background before Origen* (Washington: Catholic University of America Press, 1978). For Robert Daly's study of biblical sacrifice in relation to the theory of René Girard, see *Sacrifice Unveiled: The True Meaning of Christian Sacrifice* (London: Bloomsbury, 2009).

On the meaning of sacrifice in the Old Testament, see Roger T. Beckwith and Martin J. Selman, editors, *Sacrifice in the Bible* (Carlisle, UK: Paternoster Press, 1995); Mary Douglas, *Leviticus as Literature* (Oxford: Oxford University Press, 1999); George Buchanan Gray, *Sacrifice in the Old Testament: Its Theory and Practice* (New York: Ktav, 1971); Ithamar Gruenwald, *Rituals and Ritual Theory in Ancient Israel* (Leiden: Brill, 2003); Moshe Halbertal, *On Sacrifice* (Princeton: Princeton University Press, 2012); and Rolf Rendtorff and Robert A. Kugler, editors, *The Book of Leviticus: Composition and Reception* (Leiden: Brill, 2003).

Girard sharply contrasts the meaning of sacrifice in the Old Testament and the New Testament. For views stressing continuity in biblical sacrifice, see Bruce Chilton and Craig A. Evans, *Jesus in Context: Temple, Purity, and Restoration* (Leiden: Brill, 1997); Bruce Chilton, *The Temple of Jesus: His Sacrificial Program within a Cultural History of Sacrifice* (University Park, PA: Pennsylvania State University Press, 1992); Mary Douglas, "The Eucharist: Its Continuity with the Bread Sacrifice of Leviticus," *Catholicism and Catholicity: Eucharistic Communities in Historical and Contemporary Perspectives*, edited by Sarah Beckwith (Oxford: Basil Blackwell, 1999); Jonathan Klawans, *Purity, Sacrifice, and the Temple: Symbolism and Supersessionism in the Study of Ancient Judaism* (Oxford: Oxford University Press, 2006); and Raymund Schwager, *Jesus in the Drama of Salvation: Toward a Biblical Doctrine of Redemption*, translated by James G. Williams (New York: Crossroad Publishers, 1999).

For a critique of Girard's interpretation of the scapegoat ritual, see Mary Douglas, "The Go-Away Goat," in *The Book of Leviticus*, edited by Rolf Rentorff and Robert Kugler (Leiden: Brill, 2003): 121–141. On the meaning of the binding of Isaac, see Louis Arthur Berman, *The Akedah: The Binding of Isaac* (Northvale, NJ: Aronson Press, 1997) and Edward Noort and Eibert J. C. Tigchelaar, editors, *The Sacrifice of Isaac: The Aqedah, Genesis 22 and Its Interpretations* (Leiden: Brill, 2002).

On sacrifice and scapegoats in other cultures, see Jan Bremmer, "Scapegoat Rituals in Ancient Greece," *Harvard Studies in Classical Philology* (1983): 299–320; Walter Burkert, *Homo Necans: The Anthropology of Ancient Greek Sacrificial Ritual and Myth*, translated by

Peter Bing (Berkeley: University of California Press, 1983); and Luc de Heusch, *Sacrifice in Africa: A Structuralist Approach* (Bloomington: Indiana University Press, 1985).

For some critical appraisals of Girard's reading of the Bible in general, see James Alison, *The Joy of Being Wrong: Original Sin Through Easter Eyes* (New York: Crossroad, 1998); Ann W. Astell and Sandor Goodhart, *Sacrifice, Scripture, and Substitution: Readings in Ancient Judaism and Christianity* (Notre Dame, IN: University of Notre Dame Press, 2011); Michael Kirwan, *Girard and Theology* (London: T. and T. Clark, 2009); Leo D. Lefebure, *Revelation, the Religions, and Violence* (Maryknoll, NY: Orbis, 2000); William Lloyd Newell, *Desire in René Girard and Jesus* (Lanham, MD: Lexington, 2012); Raymund Schwager, *Must There Be Scapegoats? Violence and Redemption in the Bible*, translated by Maria L. Assad (New York: Harper and Row, 1989); Lucien Scubla, "The Christianity of René Girard and the Nature of Religion," *Violence and Truth: On the Work of René Girard*, edited by Paul Dumouchel (London: Athlone, 1987); and James G. Williams, *The Bible, Violence, and the Sacred: Liberation from the Myth of Sanctioned Violence* (New York: Harper Collins, 1991).

Concluding Reflections on Violence

For some totally contradictory theories of violence, see Hannah Arendt, *On Violence* (New York: Harcourt Brace, and World, 1970); M. K. Gandhi, *Non-Violent Resistance (Satyagraha)* (New York: Schocken Books, 1951); Frantz Fanon, *The Wretched of the Earth*, translated by Richard Philcox (New York: Grove Press, 2005); Georges Sorel, *Reflections on Violence*, edited by Jeremy Jennings (Cambridge: Cambridge University Press, 1999); and Bruce B. Lawrence and Aisha Karim, editors, *On Violence: A Reader* (Durham, NC: Duke University Press, 2007).

On religion as a cause of violence, see Hector Avalos, *Fighting Words: The Origins of Religious Violence* (Amherst, NY: Prometheus, 2005); David A. Bernat and Jonathan Klawans, editors, *Religion and Violence: The Biblical Heritage* (Sheffield: Sheffield Phoenix, 2007); Jennifer L. Jefferis, *Religion and Political Violence: Sacred Protest in the Modern World* (London: Routledge, 2010); Mark Juergensmeyer, editor, *Violence and the Sacred in the Modern World* (London: Frank Cass, 1991) and *Terror in the Mind of God: The Global Rise of Religious Violence* (Berkeley: University of California Press, 2003); and Regina Schwartz, *The Curse of Cain: The Violent Legacy of Monotheism* (Chicago: University of Chicago Press, 1997).

Acknowledgments

I was introduced to the thought of René Girard by the late Professor Donald Sheehan of Dartmouth College, who led an Orthodox Christian reading group. I have learned a great deal about Girard from conversations with Professor Michael Kirwan, S.J., and from correspondence with Professor Robert Daly, S.J., Professor Paisley Livingston, Professor Jacob Howland, Professor Stephen Gardner, and Professor John Ranieri. I want to thank Professors Robert Daly and John Milbank for generously allowing me to use their names for characters in the dialogue of Chapter Five. "Robert Daly" in my dialogue presents the arguments from his classic books on sacrifice from the 1970s; my "John Milbank" is broadly inspired by the work of John Milbank, but I do not attempt to present his arguments on sacrifice in any detail. I am also very indebted to my research assistants Michelle Gil, Jessica Tong, and Joseph Torsella. Yevgenia Rem deserves special thanks for her invaluable assistance in research as well as in copyediting. I blame the highly unorthodox structure of these dialogues on the literary passions of my wife, Kirsten Giebutowski. No one has taught me to appreciate Girard's insights more than my late mentor and friend, Joseph Daschbach. I dedicate this book to his memory.

Printed and bound by CPI Group (UK) Ltd, Croydon, CR0 4YY

09/06/2025

14685823-0004